SEP 14

READING

the love of learning,
the sequestered nooks,
and all the sweet serenity of books.
— Longfellow —

PIES + CAKE
STORYTIME
CATS
DOGS
COOKBOOK

STORIES
CHRISTMAS
HOLIDAYS
STARS

This Book Belongs
to

Christmas

Book 16

Christmas

Gooseberry Patch

Wishing all our family & friends the
happiest of holidays!

Our Story

Back in 1984, we were next-door neighbors raising our families in the little town of Delaware, Ohio. Two moms with small children, we were looking for a way to do what we loved and stay home with the kids too. We had always shared a love of home cooking and making memories with family & friends and so, after many a conversation over the backyard fence, Gooseberry Patch was born.

We put together our first catalog at our kitchen tables, enlisting the help of our loved ones wherever we could. From that very first mailing, we found an immediate connection with many of our customers and it wasn't long before we began receiving letters, photos and recipes from these new friends. In 1992, we put together our very first cookbook, compiled from hundreds of these recipes and, the rest, as they say, is history.

Hard to believe it's been over 25 years since those kitchen-table days! From that original little Gooseberry Patch family, we've grown to include an amazing group of creative folks who love cooking, decorating and creating as much as we do. Today, we're best known for our homestyle, family-friendly cookbooks, now recognized as national bestsellers.

One thing's for sure, we couldn't have done it without our friends all across the country. Each year, we're honored to turn thousands of your recipes into our collectible cookbooks. Our hope is that each book captures the stories and heart of all of you who have shared with us. Whether you've been with us since the beginning or are just discovering us, welcome to the Gooseberry Patch family!

We couldn't make our best-selling cookbooks without YOU!

Each of our books is filled with recipes from cooks just like you, gathered from kitchens all across the country.

Share your tried & true recipes with us on our website and you could be selected for an upcoming cookbook. If your recipe is included, you'll receive a FREE copy of the cookbook when it's published!

www.gooseberrypatch.com

We'd love to add YOU to our Circle of Friends!

Get free recipes, crafts, giveaways and so much more when you join our email club...join us online at all the spots below for even more goodies!

Deck the Halls..............................8
Decorate your home all through the house with festive crafts and trims.

Share the Spirit...........................18
Create handmade gifts this year that will please everyone on your Christmas list.

A Woodland Holiday.....................24
Bring a little of the outdoors inside to create a nature-inspired holiday.

Perfectly Plaid...........................30
Use the traditional pattern of plaid in your holiday decorating this season.

Simplify the Season....................38
It is never too late to make the season sparkle when you make easy-does-it projects.

Farmhouse-Style Christmas.....................44
Celebrate farmhouse-style with down-home crafts and decorations.

Santa's Little Helpers.....................56
Let the little ones help make the holiday even more special.

Who would guess that yards of yarn can be transformed into a sweet little Pom-pom Garland to adorn your holiday tree? The handmade pom-poms are tied to purchased ball fringe for the soft and full look. Friendly Retro Reindeer seem to enjoy each other as they are tucked into a fresh evergreen tree. The little fellows are created by layering felt and formed around light cardboard.

Pom-pom Garland

Almost like magic, lengths of yarn wrapped around and around create soft little balls of fluff that combine to make a sweet holiday garland for your tree.

- purchased ball fringe yardage in desired length and colors
- 3 skeins of cotton yarn in desired colors
- 12" ruler or stick that measures about 1" wide
- tape
- scissors

1. Cut a 12" length of yarn from desired color of yarn. Lay the yarn the long way across the ruler or stick and tape the yarn at each end. See photo on page 128.
2. Find the end of the yarn on the skein, and begin wrapping the yarn around and around at the middle of the ruler. **Note:** To make a full pom-pom it takes about 75 wraps per pom-pom depending on the type of yarn chosen.
3. Remove the tape from the long piece of yarn. Pull yarn tightly around the wrapped yarn and tie with a double knot.

(continued on page 128)

Pom-pom Garland

Pom-pom Package Trim

Friendly Retro Reindeer

Drawing inspiration from vintage needlework designs, these cheery deer will make your guests smile. Layers of felt are strengthened by an invisible slip of cardboard. The little fellows are stitched with simple whip and straight stitches. A pom-pom nose and bright red bow add charm and whimsy.

Dimensions: 6¼ " h x 5" w
(at nose)

- felt such as National Nonwovens: caramel, tan, white, red
- lightweight cardboard (can be from cereal or cracker box)
- white pom-poms
- 9" leather cording
- embroidery floss in tan and black
- sewing and embroidery needles
- scissors

1. Use the template patterns (page 155) as your guide to cut the deer pieces out of felt and cardboard. Cut 2 body pieces and one head piece out of caramel, a chest piece and eye piece out of tan, a white tail piece, and a ribbon and bow out of red. Or, cut from desired colors. Cut the body insert, which is smaller than the body, out of cardboard.
2. Position and stitch the head, eyepiece, chest and tail to the top deer piece. Pin the smaller pieces to the top deer piece. Use a single strand of tan floss and small stitches to sew the head, eyepiece, chest and tail piece in place.

(continued on page 128)

Friendly
Retro Reindeer

Lacy Snowflakes

Remember, no two will ever be alike!

- vintage sheet music, music-print scrapbook paper or copyright-free sheet music
- copy machine (optional)
- vellum in white or off-white (optional)
- 8" length of narrow ribbon
- crafts glue
- sharp scissors
- decorative paper punch (optional)

1. Choose the desired paper to make the snowflakes. The paper should not be too heavy, or it will be hard to cut. You can use actual sheets of vintage music. If copying the music to vellum, be sure the music is copyright-free.

(continued on page 129)

Music-Inspired Paper Chain

Instructions are on page 128.

Lacy Snowflakes

Music-Inspired Paper Chain

Lacy Snowflakes

Gingham & Felt Mini Trees

Make these sweet little trees by lining quilt scraps with sturdy felts and stitching them on your machine right side out. Dress them up by trimming with an assortment of new and vintage buttons.

Dimensions:
Large: 10$\frac{1}{2}$" high x 5" base
Medium: 9" high x 4" base
Small: 8" high x 3$\frac{1}{2}$" base

- cotton fabric: gingham, calicos, dotted, florals
- wool felt such as National Nonwovens 30% Woolfelt: 2 shades of green and white

- assorted $\frac{1}{4}$" to 1" buttons: ivory, white, blue, red, green
- polyester fiberfill
- off-white thread
- rotary cutter, straight edge and cutting matt
- scissors
- pinking shears
- sewing machine
- hot-glue gun and glue sticks
- circle templates

(continued on page 129)

Lacy Snowflakes are folded and cut to look like 3-D pieces of nature's art. Strips of paper are curled to make a Music-Inspired Paper Chain. Gingham & Felt Mini Trees are stuffed to stand tall on any mantel or country cupboard.

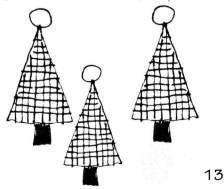

Gingham & Felt Mini Trees

13

Christmas Carol Table Runner

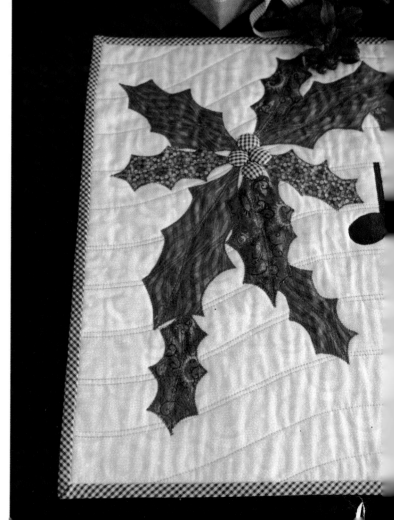

Christmas Carol Table Runner

Fa la la la la...this beautiful table runner will become a happy and beautiful addition to your holiday decorating!

Dimensions: 16" x 32"
Use $1/4$" seam allowances and 40" w fabric

- $1/2$ yard light caramel textured print (for background)
- 3 fat quarters (medium, medium/dark, dark) green cotton prints (for holly leaves)
- 1 fat quarter dark red cotton print (for notes)
- $1/2$ yard red tiny woven check gingham or print (for berries and binding)
- $2/3$ yard coordinating cotton print (for backing)
- 1 yard paper-backed fusible web
- 19" x 34" piece of quilt batting

Cut the Quilt Pieces
1. From the background fabric cut a 17" x 33" rectangle.
2. From the red check fabric cut five $2^{1}/4$" bias strips for binding.
3. From the backing fabric cut a 18" x 34" rectangle.

(continued on page 130)

Appliqué a Christmas Carol Table Runner that is sure to become a treasured work of art. The holly leaves and musical notes are tone-on-tone prints that gracefully lay on the piece. Tiny stuffed gingham circles become the berries. Fresh little trees are an Evergreen Welcome when placed in country-style pails adorned with checked ribbon.

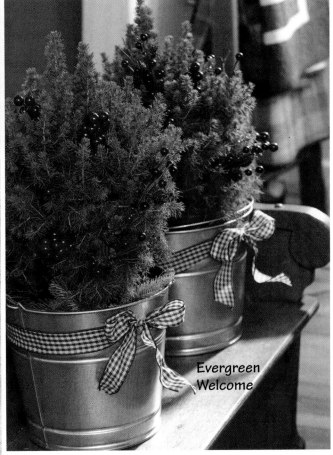

Evergreen
Welcome

Evergreen Welcome
Instructions are on page 131.

Whip up a Rickrack Place Mat in no time for everyone at your holiday table. The pretty little place mat is adorned with large rickrack. Purchased square candles take on a new light when they are carved to become Carved Evergreen Candles. Make them the centerpiece at your holiday table. Sweet Music Napkin Rings are upbeat and quick to make!

Rickrack Place Mat

Pieces of rickrack are couched onto a felt place mat to make a quick and festive addition to your holiday table.

- $^1/_2$ yard felt such as National Nonwovens in strawberry red
- $1^1/_4$ yard large red rickrack
- straight pins
- matching sewing thread
- ivory embroidery floss
- scissors

1. Cut felt to 14" x 19" piece. Fold 1" to the front around all sides, pinning in place. Lightly press in place.
2. Fold corner in to miter, cutting out bulk. Hand stitch mitered corners using matching sewing thread.
3. Pin the rickrack to the place mat, placing rickrack over cut edge. Stitch rickrack to felt backing using 3 strands of ivory embroidery floss. Stitch by taking a long stitch over the center of the rickrack, and a very small stitch through the felt to the other side of the rickrack for the second long stitch. Press finished mat.

Rickrack Place Mat

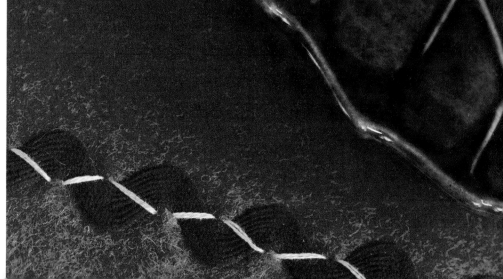

Carved Evergreen Candles

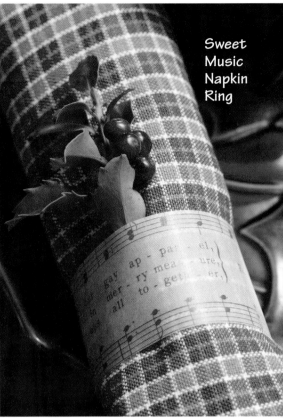

Sweet Music Napkin Ring
A tiny piece of sheet music is cut along the bar line to make a very sweet napkin ring in no time!

- vintage sheet music, music-print scrapbook paper or copyright-free sheet music
- copy machine (optional)
- vellum in white or off-white
- scissors
- crafts glue

1. Using the desired paper, cut the music along the bar lines revealing the notes and words on the music. Cut the piece about 7" long.
2. Wrap the paper around to form a loop and glue at the back. Let dry. Slide onto rolled napkin.

Carved Evergreen Candles
Just a little carving using a linoleum tool transforms a simple candle into a piece of holiday art.

- purchased square green candle
- pencil
- linoleum cutter tool set
- paintbrush
- soft cloth

1. Wipe off the candle with a soft cloth. Referring to the photo, above, mark the design on the candle. Or, freehand the design.
2. Choose the desired blade from the linoleum cutter set. Making sure to carve AWAY from you, carve in the design. As you carve, use a dry paintbrush to dust away any wax.
3. When finished carving, wipe with soft cloth.

Remember when you would wish for something very special for Christmas and then be amazed when it appeared under the tree? Handmade gifts are the best gifts of all! They can be personalized to fit a special color scheme or size. Stitch a Cheery Cherry Tote Bag for that shopper on your list. Then make that little one happy with an appliqué Yummy First Foods Bib and a Foxy Baby Hat. Make a special bracelet just for Grandma using her favorite colors or a Chalkboard Message Board for that busy neighbor. Need some ideas for wrapping these special gifts? Try a Buttons and Bows Wrap or felt Christmas motifs to dress up your packages. Whatever you choose to make, your gifts will be cherished for the thought you gave to each and every one!

Share the Spirit

Cheery Cherry Tote Bag Instructions are on page 131.

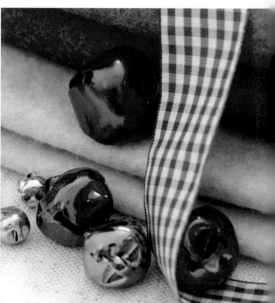

Cheery Cherry Tote Bag

Yummy First Foods Bib

He'll keep his little Christmas outfit clean and dry when he wears this sweet little bib!

- tissue paper
- transfer paper or pen
- scissors
- $\frac{1}{2}$ yard muslin fabric
- $\frac{1}{2}$ yard print fabric (for backing)
- $\frac{1}{2}$ yard lightweight batting
- $\frac{1}{4}$ yard of fusible interfacing
- $\frac{1}{4}$ yard of stripe fabric (for bib binding)
- scraps of solid color and print fabrics for appliqué pieces
- embroidery floss, DMC colors: 905, 936, 921, 937
- embroidery needle
- matching sewing thread
- adhesive fastener tape such as Velcro

1. Enlarge and copy the patterns (page 147) onto tissue paper and cut out. Copy the bib pattern onto the muslin and cut out. Transfer the writing onto the muslin bib front.

2. Cut another bib shape from the print fabric for the bib back. Cut

Yummy First Foods Bib

one bib shape from the lightweight batting. Set aside.

3. Choose the fabrics for the food appliqués. Iron a small piece of each color of fabric to one side of the fusible webbing. Transfer the food patterns to the front of the fused fabric. Cut out.

4. Fuse the 3 food patterns to the muslin bib front referring to the pattern placement.

(continued on page 131)

He'll gobble up his healthy fruits and veggies when he wears the Yummy First Foods Bib you make him! The piece has simple appliqué shapes that are embellished with embroidery stitches. Crochet a Foxy Baby Hat in no time using just two basic crochet stitches.

Foxy Baby Hat

He will look adorable wearing his little fox hat! The hat is designed using only 3 colors of yarn and works up quickly!

Skill Level: beginner
Size: 4 to 8 months
Circumference: 18"
Gauge: 3 stitches per inch

- Red Heart acrylic yarn: 7 oz. ball: 1 each of orange, light grey and dark grey
- size K crochet hook
- sewing needle large enough to accommodate yarn

ABBREVIATIONS

ch=chain
sl st=slip stitch
st=stitch
sts=stitches
sc=single crochet
hdc=half double crochet
dc=double crochet
dec=decrease
beg=beginning

(continued on page 132)

Foxy Baby Hat

Grandmother's Beaded Bracelet

Choose the colors that she loves, or use pink for little girls and blue for little boys to make this sparkling beaded bracelet.

- piece of felt (optional)
- beading wire
- clasp set in desired style
- glass beads in desired colors or birthstone colors
- charms in desired colors and shapes
- 2 crimp beads
- crimping tool
- wire cutters

1. Plan the design for the bracelet by laying the beads and charms in the order to be strung. If desired, lay the beads on a piece of felt to keep them from rolling.

2. Cut the beading wire to the desired length, allowing for bending the wire at both ends to secure the clasps.

3. Slide a crimp bead onto the wire end, through one end of the clasp, and back through the crimp bead, leaving about $\frac{1}{2}$"of the wire tail.

(continued on page 132)

Buttons & Bows Wraps

Instructions start on page 132.

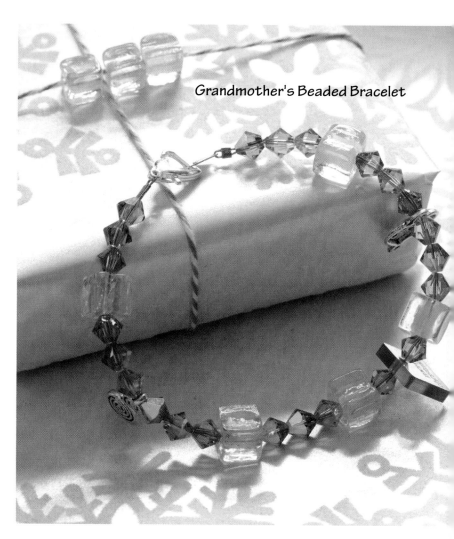

Grandmother's Beaded Bracelet

Button & Bows Wraps

Chalkboard Message Board

Felt Package Toppers

Chalkboard Message Board

Keeping track of the holiday events will be easy for the lucky recipient of this clever chalkboard message center!

- purchased wood cutting board
- tracing paper
- pencil
- scissors
- chalkboard paint
- small paintbrush
- 12" length of 1" w ribbon
- colored chalk

Note: *Do not use for food after making into the message board.*

1. Enlarge and copy the tree pattern (page 146) onto tracing paper. Cut out.
2. Be sure that the cutting board is clean and dry. Trace around the tree shape on to the front of the cutting board.
3. Using the chalkboard paint, carefully paint in the tree area. Use two coats if necessary to get a smooth finish. Let dry.
4. Use colored chalk to make designs on the tree. Tie a ribbon through the top of the board.

Felt Package Toppers
Instructions are on page 133.

Make a Grandmother's Beaded Bracelet that she will always treasure! A little twine and buttons make Buttons & Bows Wraps. What fun to create a Chalkboard Message Board using a purchased cutting board. Christmas motifs cut from felt make pretty Felt Package Toppers.

Let the beauty of nature be the inspiration for your decorating theme this holiday season. Cranberry reds, cedar greens, tree bark brown and winter whites make the color palette easy to follow. Start by making glass-like Icy Wreaths to hang on the branches outside your window. Then paint some Message Rocks and present them in a little basket by your door. How about forming some sweet mushrooms using oven-bake clay and using them to surround a birch bark log that holds red tapered candles? Evergreen Print Greeting Cards are so easy and fun to make, you can make dozens to send to your nature-loving friends. So let heaven and nature sing with the crafts you make and decorating ideas you share this Christmas.

A Woodland Holiday

Icy Wreaths

Icy Wreaths are fun and almost magical to make. A Sticks & Stones Swag combines nature's finds for a stunning look. Create a traditional Buche De Noel using a birch log and candles.

Icy Wreaths

Bits of greenery, fresh cranberries and fruit slices combine to make stunning ice wreaths to decorate the outside of your holiday home.

- metal round pan such as a pie plate or cake pan
- small plastic drinking glass
- fresh cranberries, bits of greenery, sliced apples, small pieces of orange peel
- water
- twine

1. Place the pan on a flat surface and set the glass in the middle of the pan. Fill glass with water. See photo, below.
2. Arrange the fruits and greenery around the glass. Fill the pan with water. Set the pan outside if the temperature is below 32 degrees or in a freezer. Freeze until frozen.
3. Remove the glass and frozen ring from pan. Wrap twine around the top of ice wreath to hang.

Sticks & Stones Swag
Instructions are on page 133.

Sticks & Stones Swag

Buche De Noel

Buche De Noel

Cheery red polymer clay mushrooms punctuate fresh evergreen and evoke the magic of the woods.

- birch log
- saw
- drill
- waxed paper
- glass baking dish
- polymer clay in red and white
- spoon (optional)
- baking dish; oven
- 4 red taper candles
- fresh evergreen pieces

(continued on page 133)

Deer Sachet

Owl Sachet

Bunny Sachet

Woodland Sachets

These little sachets are not only pretty to look at... they smell divine. The fresh sweet scent of lavender and balsam brings peace and happiness.

- balsam/lavender herb mix
- muslin
- tan gingham cotton
- felt such as National Nonwovens: green red, tan, rose and brown
- embroidery floss in red and green
- embroidery needle
- scissors

1. Cut muslin and gingham rectangles for the sachets' front and backs. Cut both muslin and gingham into 4" x 6$\frac{1}{2}$" rectangles for each sachet.

2. Use the template patterns (page 154) to cut the animal silhouettes out of the colored felt. Cut an animal silhouette out of the tan, rose or brown felt. Cut $\frac{3}{8}$" circle berries out of red felt and the leaf template out of green felt.

(continued on page 134)

Deck the Halls

Friendly Retro Reindeer snuggle with soft, fluffy pom-poms on a Christmas tree that decks the halls with holiday cheer. Crisp, Lacy Snowflakes surprise the eye with 3-D folding and decorative edges. The season is all aglow with Carved Evergreen Candles perched on red vintage candle stands. Gingham & Felt Mini Trees align on a country cupboard, and the table is set with holly dishes upon a Rickrack Place Mat. An heirloom quality Christmas Carol Table Runner decorates the dining room for family & friends that come to call. The holiday house is decked out for Christmas, and you are ready to celebrate the merriest time of the year!

Wrapped-Up Gifts from the Kitchen........64
Treat them to yummy gifts from the kitchen!

Cozy Christmas Eve Supper...................80
Cuddle up for some Christmas Eve goodies you'll love to make and share.

Holiday Cupcakes by the Dozen.............88
Frosted, sugared, piped and sprinkled. . .you'll have fun making all kinds of cupcakes!

Dinner at Grandma's! 96
Over the river and through the woods. . .for some favorite comfort foods!

Festive Breads and Muffins..................106
Breads and muffins warm and fresh from the oven. . .what could be better?

Sweet Desserts....................................112
Everyone loves a little sugar at Christmastime!

Party Favorites 120
Gather together to celebrate the best time of year with easy party goodies!

Project Instructions 128

General Instructions..........143

Patterns...............................146

Crafts/Recipe Index 158

Credits.................................160

Perfectly Plaid

Spruce up your Christmas decorating with traditional holiday plaid fabrics and designs. Start by choosing everyone's favorite. . . cozy red-plaid flannel! Stitch it into a stocking that Santa will love to fill! Snippets of flannel with pinked edges become a Fluffy Flannel Wreath and warm tones of flannel become a Flannel Tree Trio. Argyle is the pattern for a colorful holiday pillow and paper tape layers create a plaid design on a purchased box. Love to paint? Try using glass paints on a pretty glass vase to make a plaid design that is almost magical. Whatever you choose to make, let a pretty plaid design become your favorite holiday pattern this year!

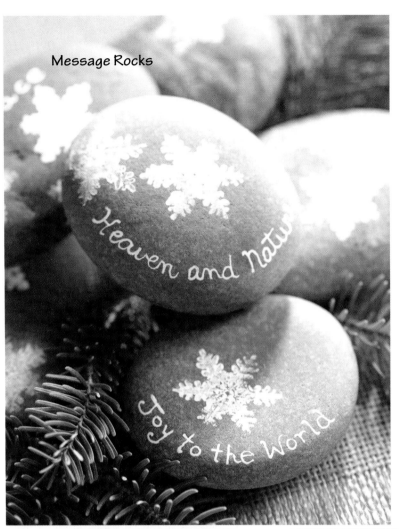

Message Rocks

Mix up a batch of dried herbs and cut multiple fabric rectangles and felt silhouettes to make Woodland Sachets. Message Rocks are lovely to read and to hold. Evergreen Print Greeting Cards are so easy to make you'll want to make dozens to send.

Message Rocks
Let nature help send the messages you want to share this holiday season.

• smooth flat rocks
• small rubber stamp
• acrylic paint in desired colors
• disposable plate
• fine-line white permanent marker

1. Be sure the rocks are clean and dry. Using just a little paint on the plate, dip the rubber stamp in the paint and stamp the rocks. Let dry.
2. Use the fine-line white marker to write holiday words and messages on the rocks.

Evergreen Print Greeting Cards
Instructions are on page 134.

Evergreen Print Greeting Cards

Red-Plaid Flannel Stocking

A Red-Plaid Flannel Stocking, a Cable Sweater Stocking and a Pom-Pom Cuff Stocking all use the plaid motif to make their holiday statements! Whip up a Fluffy Flannel Wreath in no time using little squares of plaid flannel.

Cable Sweater Stocking

A castaway sweater with a lovely cable design takes on new life as a stunning Christmas stocking. The cuff is adorned with a big plaid covered button.

- old sweater with cable pattern
- $1/2$ yard white fabric with light body or stiffness for lining
- scrap of flannel for button cover
- large button cover kit
- $2^1/3$x7" strip of flannel fabric for loop
- matching sewing thread
- scissors
- sewing machine

1. Enlarge the pattern (page 156) and cut out. Wash, dry and iron the sweater. Treating the sweater as fabric, lay the patterns on the sweater and cut out the pattern pieces from the desired areas of the sweater reversing one of the body shapes. Repeat for the lining pieces.

Cable Sweater Stocking
Pom-Pom Cuff Stocking

2. Sew the stocking front to the stocking back with right sides together, using $3/8$" seams and leaving the top edge open. Trim the seams, and clip curves. Turn the stocking right side out. Press.
3. Repeat with lining fabric except do not turn right side out. Trim seams to reduce bulk in stocking.

Insert lining inside turned sweater stocking, keeping top straight edges even.

(continued on page 135)

Pom-Pom Cuff Stocking and Red-Plaid Flannel Stocking
Instructions are on page 135.

Fluffy Flannel Wreath

2. Fold each square in half and in half again to find the middle. Place the pin at that point and pin to the wreath form. Continue pinning the small squares to the form until the desired fullness is achieved.

3. Thread a piece of embroidery floss through the holes in the buttons. Tie in the back. Hot-glue the buttons atop each other. Hot-glue to the top of the wreath.

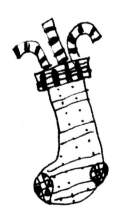

Fluffy Flannel Wreath

Little squares of plaid flannel are tucked together to make a sweet and soft wreath for Christmas decorating. Vintage buttons grouped and glued together make a focal point for this festive decoration.

• purchased 12" foam wreath form such as Styrofoam
• ¹/₂ yard flannel *each* in two different prints and colors

• pinking shears
• straight pins
• embroidery floss in desired colors
• vintage buttons
• hot-glue gun and glue sticks

1. Press flannel. Use pinking shears to cut approximately 50 3"x3" squares of the desired patterns and colors of flannel.

Argyle Sweater Pillow

Make good use of a favorite old sweater by transforming it into a delightful pillow for the holidays. The pillow size will be determined by the placement and size of the pattern on the castaway sweater.

- castaway argyle sweater
- $^1/_2$ yard fabric for ruffle
- $^1/_2$ yard check fabric for ruffle trim
- $^1/_2$ yard of lining fabric
- polyester fiberfill batting
- scissors
- matching sewing thread
- sewing machine

1. Note: *the size of the pillow is determined by the size of the pattern area on the pillow.*
Cut the pattern area square from the sweater. Cut another piece the same size from the sweater for the back of the sweater. Cut lining pieces to match sweater squares. Baste the lining to the front and back pieces being careful not to stretch the sweater pieces. Set aside.

2. Cut the ruffle trim 4" w x the width of the fabric creating strips. Cut the check fabric 2"w x the width of the fabric creating strips.

3. Stitch short ends of strips together. Press seams open. Press long lengths in half.

4. Create pleats by stitching with basting stitch close to raw edge of ruffle strip. Tuck a pinch of fabric under presser foot at 1" intervals to create pleats. Stitch check print to pleated ruffle having raw edges together. Baste in place.

5. Pin ruffle strips to sweater front, right sides together. Stitch with ½" seam to secure. Lay back of sweater over front with right sides together. Pin. Stitch with ½" seam leaving an opening for turning pillow.

6. Turn pillow right side out and press ruffle pleats. Fill with pillow insert or loose batting. Whip stitch the opening closed.

Argyle Sweater Pillow

1. Be sure the boxes are clean and dry. Use the ruler and pencil to plan the design, marking at top and bottom where tape is to be placed. **2.** Cut the tape to fit the boxes and place the tape both horizontally and vertically, overlapping the tape to make a plaid design. Press down tape to secure.

A favorite old sweater turns into a beautiful Argyle Sweater Pillow with just a little trimming and tucking. Pretty Plaid Boxes are a snap to make when you use paper tape in the colors that fit your holiday decorating scheme.

Pretty Plaid Boxes

Purchased drawers or painted boxes become handy catch-alls for your holiday crafting supplies. Give each drawer or box its own personality with some printed paper tape that you overlap to create plaid designs.

- painted or purchased drawers or boxes
- ruler
- pencil
- paper tape such as Washi tape
- scissors

Flannel Tree Trio

These darling rustic trees are quick and simple to whip up. Recycle old flannel shirts and pj's or purchase an assortment of flannel plaids. Strengthen the fabric with adhesive fleece lining before stitching the pattern pieces together. Natural sticks make instant tree trunks. Trim the finished tree with metal bells and a suede bow. They look pretty hanging in a window, on a cabinet knob or on a tree branch.

- $1/4$ yard flannel plaid in 3 different colors
- $1/4$ yard fusible fleece such as Heat 'n Bond
- $1/4$" small metal jingle bells
- 4" long sticks
- $6^{1}/2$" length of leather cording for hanger
- suede lace for decorative bows
- hot-glue gun and glue sticks
- matching sewing thread
- scissors
- sewing machine

(continued on page 135)

Flannel Tree Trio

Painted Plaid Vase

Tiny jingle bells and tiny suede bows adorn the Flannel Tree Trio that hangs on a fresh evergreen tree. Get out those glass paints to make a Painted Plaid Vase. . .clearly a lovely addition to your holiday decorating.

- soft cloth
- glass paints in desired colors
- masking tape
- scissors
- paintbrush

1. Be sure the container is clean and dry. Use a soft cloth to wipe off the container with rubbing alcohol and let dry.
2. Use masking tape to mask off stripes running in one direction. Paint with glass paints and let dry.
3. Mask over those stripes (carefully masking over the painted area). Paint with another color. Let dry.
4. Continue to mask the other stripes (carefully masking over the painted areas) and paint over the previous stripes creating a plaid look. Let dry. Follow manufacturer's directions for curing paint.

Painted Plaid Vase

Painting stripes of color atop one another creates a plaid design on a clear glass vase or dish.

- clear glass square-shaped vase or container
- rubbing alcohol

simplify the Season

Christmas is just around the corner, but there is plenty of time to decorate your home and still enjoy the holidays! Purchased pillows can bring musical messages when you add your own handwriting. Still want to make your own Christmas cards? You'll have time to make dozens of Easy Sticker Cards using pre-folded cards and holiday stickers. Candles add warmth and holiday glow to your home, and a Bracelet Candle Centerpiece can be created in minutes! Clever Christmas Package Bookends add an unexpected bit of Christmas cheer to your bookcases. So catch your breath, sit back and sip that hot chocolate. You've decorated your beautiful holiday home . . .just in the nick of time!

Have yourself a Merry Little Christmas

Lyrical Pillows

Purchased pillows become works of art when they display your favorite Christmas carol lyrics. Add a set of jingle bells and you have created a lovely Christmas addition to your holiday decorating in no time!

- purchased cotton pillow preferably with lines on the design
- plain white paper the size of the pillow
- gray permanent marker
- 3 small to medium-size jingle bells
- ribbon in desired width and color
- needle
- sewing thread to match pillow

1. Plan the design for the pillow by practicing the writing on a plain sheet of paper the same size as the pillow. Use the gray marker to write the desired words on the pillow.
2. Group the jingle bells together and sew to the pillow corner. Tie a bow using the ribbon and stitch above the jingle bells.

Easy Sticker Cards
Instructions are on page 136.

Lyrical Pillows

Easy Sticker Cards

Create your own set of Lyrical Pillows by writing your favorite Christmas tune on the pillow using a permanent marker. Purchased bracelets make a Bracelet Candle Centerpiece easy and simple to make. Making your own Christmas cards is fun but it can take so much time. This year, make Easy Sticker Cards in the blink of an eye.

Bracelet Candle Centerpiece

Purchased bracelets make creating a centerpiece super easy!

- 3 candles in desired colors
- 3 beaded bracelets in desired colors
- rectangular shaped dish to hold candles
- holly twigs or evergreen

1. Arrange the candles on the dish. Slide the bracelets on the candles having them rest about halfway down on the candle.
2. Cut pieces of holly or evergreen and tuck around the candles.

Never leave a burning candle unattended.

Christmas Package Bookends will have your guests looking twice at your bookshelf. Simply weight the packages and let them support your favorite books! Candles add warmth and glow to the holidays! Whether you want to make a Vintage Button Candle, Popcorn Candles or a Christmas Lights Candle, these Clever Candle Surrounds will make your holiday table twinkle with the Christmas spirit.

Christmas Package Bookends

Christmas Package Bookends
Let little packages earn their place on the bookshelf by serving as clever little bookends for your favorite books.

- small gift boxes: one smaller than the other
- bag of rice
- ribbon
- hot-glue gun and glue sticks

1. Fill the gift boxes with rice and hot-glue the boxes closed.
2. Wrap the gift boxes as desired coordinating the colors on the boxes. Wrap ribbon around the larger box but do not tie a bow.
3. Wrap a ribbon around the smaller box and tie a bow at the top.
4. Hot-glue the smaller box atop the larger box. Set the box set against the books.

Vintage Button Candle

Christmas Lights Candle

Popcorn Candles

Clever Candle Surrounds

Candles give a warm glow to the holiday season and find their places on tables, mantels and cupboards. Choose the colors and styles of candles that you like and then surround them with colorful and sometimes unexpected items.

- candles in desired colors and sizes
- small candle holders for smaller candles
- vessel or dish to hold candle and surrounding items
- vintage buttons, Christmas light bulbs, popped popcorn

1. Choose the vessel or dish you want to use for the candles. Be sure the dishes are clean and dry. If using small candles, place them in smaller candle holders and then into the larger dish.
2. Place the items such as buttons, Christmas light bulbs or popcorn around the candle or candles, arranging as needed. If using small candles, be sure that the candles are secure in the smaller holders before adding the items.

Never leave a burning candle unattended.

FARMHOUSE-STYLE CHRISTMAS

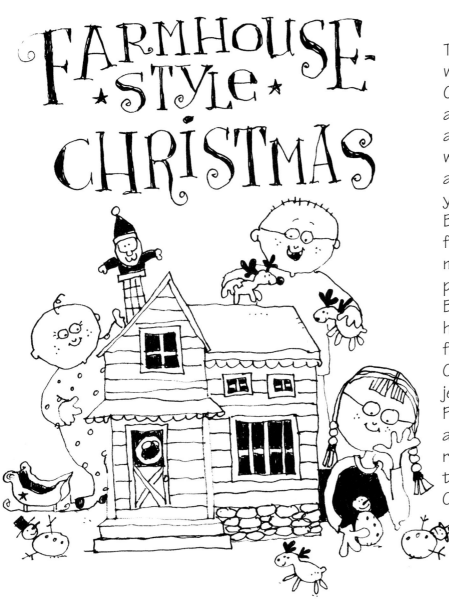

There is nothing warmer and more welcoming than a farmhouse Christmas! The mood is casual and fun with genuine smiles all around. Decorate your door with a Burlap & Berry Wreath and greet your guests wearing your Farmhouse Apron. Colorful Burlap Flower Trims make that fresh-cut Christmas tree even more festive and a ticking fabric pillow says "Merry Christmas!" Burlap-trimmed stockings are hung in hopes that Santa will find the farmhouse in time for Christmas. Those well-worn blue jeans become clever Woven Denim Place Mats embellished with just a touch of rickrack and checked ribbon. Yes, it is Christmas on the farm, and what a wonderful Christmas it is!

Burlap & Berry Wreath instructions are on page 136.

Burlap & Berry Wreath

Oil Cloth Table Topper

Oil Cloth Table Topper

Have a down-home Christmas complete with a vintage-print table cloth to showcase your home-canned goodies all wrapped up for the holidays.

- one yard of printed oil cloth (for main part of topper)
- $1/2$ yard of coordinating oil cloth (for edging)
- $1/4$ yard of checked oil cloth (for trim)
- scissors
- pinking shears
- quilt clips
- matching sewing thread

1. Cut main topper fabric to measure 36"x36".
2. Cut coordinating fabric 2" w x 40" long, cutting one long edge using pinking shears. Cut check trim fabric 1"w x 38" long, cutting one long edge using pinking shears.
3. Layer the checked trim atop the edge piece with pinked edges out leaving 1" at edge of trim piece. Treating the 2 pieces as one piece, stitch to the body piece with right sides together using $1/2$" seams. Use quilt clips to hold in place while stitching. Turn. Do not press. Cut oil cloth at corners and overlap.
4. To finish, DO NOT iron oil cloth. Lay flat or roll on cardboard roll to store.

- 1 1/2 yards oil cloth in desired pattern
- 1/4 yard checked oil cloth
- 2 yards nylon webbing
- 2 yards bias tape
- 4 yards jumbo rickrack
- scissors
- quilt clips

1. Enlarge and trace the patterns (page 149) and cut out. Draw around the pattern onto oil cloth. Cut pocket from checked oil cloth.
2. Hem top edge of pocket. Stitch rickrack over hemmed edge. Turn back edges of pocket, place on apron and topstitch in place.
3. Fold 1" under on all edges of body of apron using quilt clips to hold. Topstitch in place. Topstitch rickrack across apron top.
4. Cut bias tape and nylon webbing to length needed for neck strap and waist ties. Stitch bias tape to nylon webbing. Topstitch down center of each strap. Secure straps and ties to apron as marked on pattern.
5. Topstitch rickrack to lower edge of apron. To finish, DO NOT press oilcloth.

A colorful Oil Cloth Table Topper brings a bright farmhouse feel to your holiday decorating. Stitch a Farmhouse Apron using coordinating patterns of oil cloth trimmed in bold rickrack.

Farmhouse Apron

So practical and easy to clean, oil cloth was a favorite fabric in the mid 1900s. Making a comeback with its bright colors and patterns, oil cloth has won the hearts of modern cooks that appreciate this comfortable and colorful farmhouse style.

Burlap Flower Trims

Remember when burlap only came in a utilitarian brown color? Burlap is now such a popular fabric that it comes in all kinds of wonderful colors. Use these beautiful hues to create a bouquet of pretty flowers for your holiday tree!

For each flower:
• 10"x10" piece of burlap in desired color
• tracing paper
• pencil
• large needle
• matching sewing thread
• scissors
• contrasting button
• twine (optional)

(continued on page 136)

Burlap Flower Trims add color and dimension to your holiday tree. Make them in a rainbow of colors and set them off with a vintage button. Stitch up a Country Welcome Pillow using a vintage towel, red and white ticking fabric and bits of burlap and lace trims.

Country Welcome Pillow

*Red and white ticking fabric and a vintage
towel combine with burlap and lace for a very
welcoming pillow for the holidays.*

- vintage towel
- $1/2$ yard of red-and-white ticking
  fabric
- $1/4$ yard of gray burlap
- 1 yard of off-white lace
- matching sewing threads
- large T pin
- scrap of muslin
- "Merry Christmas" rubber stamp
- black fabric ink pad

(continued on page 136)

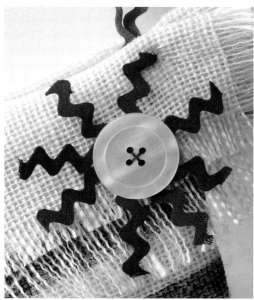

Striped Burlap Stocking

With just a little Christmas-red paint, cream colored burlap takes on a new look for the holidays.

- tracing paper
- pencil
- $1/2$ yard of cream burlap
- red fabric paint
- stencil brush
- masking tape
- $1/2$ yard of white cotton fabric (for lining)
- one large white button
- scraps of red rickrack
- scissors
- parchment paper

1. Enlarge and trace pattern (page 156) and cut out. Use the stocking pattern to cut a front and a back reversing one of the shapes. Repeat for the lining. In addition, cut a 3"x 16" piece of cream burlap for the cuff.

2. To create stripes on stocking front, position stocking front on flat surface with parchment paper under fabric. Use masking tape to secure in place.

3. Use masking tape to tape completely over the fabric leaving about 1" of fabric between masking tape pieces.

4. Using the red fabric paint and stencil brush, use an up-and-down

Striped Burlap Stocking

motion of the brush to paint the open areas created by the masking tape. Continue painting the stripes on the entire front piece. Carefully remove the masking tape. Let dry.

(continued on page 137)

Create a Striped Burlap Stocking by making your own stripes using fabric paint and masking tape. A red-and-white towel becomes the body of the stocking on this Kitchen Towel Stocking trimmed with a bright red button.

Kitchen Towel Stocking

Fringed burlap and a pretty red button make this stocking one that Santa will love!

- tracing paper
- pencil
- kitchen towel measuring at least 16"x 24"
- $1/2$ yard of white cotton fabric (for lining)
- 12"x12" piece of cream burlap
- $1/4$ yard of gray burlap
- one large red button
- scissors
- matching sewing thread

1. Enlarge and trace pattern (page 156) and cut out. Use the stocking pattern to cut a front and a back from the kitchen towel, reversing one of the shapes. Repeat for the lining using the lining fabric. In addition, cut a 6"x16" piece of gray burlap and a 5"x16" piece of cream burlap for the cuffs.

(continued on page 137)

Kitchen Towel Stocking

Woven Denim
Place Mat

Woven Denim Place Mat

Recycle old jeans and use those cool colors of denim to create a one-of-a-kind place mat for the holidays. Adding bits of rickrack and ribbon gives each place mat its own special personality.

- denim from used blue jeans in various shades of blue
- scissors
- $^1/_2$ yard backing fabric in desired print or solid
- straight pins
- trims such as rickrack or ribbon

1. Cut the jeans into flat pieces of fabric and press. Rip several strips of denim approximately $^3/_4$" to 1" w. Use different shades of denim. Cut lengths of desired trims. Lay the pieces on a flat surface. The place mat shown used about 35 strips of denim.
2. Cut a piece of backing fabric to measure 12"x18". Pin strips to one long edge of the backing piece. Pln strips to one short side of the backing piece.
3. Weave strips, one at a time, pinning each finished length as you go. Weave in rickrack and ribbons as desired. When the entire mat is woven, baste strips into place at edge. Cut the strips flush with the backing piece.
4. Rip two 12" and two 18" lengths of denim. Press in half lengthwise and stitch to each edge of the place mat for binding.

Canning Jar Candles

Canning Jar Candles

Fill those sturdy canning jars with candle wax to make candles in the colors to fit your holiday decorating scheme.

- canning jars in various sizes
- candle wax
- saucepan
- water
- tin can
- crayons with paper removed in desired colors
- length of candle wick

1. Be sure the jars are clean and dry. Suspend a length of candle wick in the empty jars. Set aside.

2. Fill the tin can with chunks of candle wax. Fill the saucepan half full of water and place the tin can in the water. Place on medium heat until water boils and the wax in the tin can begins to melt. Watch the wax carefully and heat wax only until melted.

3. Add desired color of crayon to wax until melted. Remove from heat and carefully pour the colored wax into the prepared jars. Adjust wick as necessary. Allow to set until cool.

You'll love seeing your favorite blue jeans have new life when you make them into a Woven Denim Place Mat. Canning Jar Candles are so easy to make and give a warm glow to the holiday season.

Never leave a burning candle unattended.

53

You'll be humming a tune every day of the Christmas season when you have a set of 12 Days of Christmas Kitchen Towels to display in your home. The embroidery is simple to do and the result most impressive.

12 Days of Christmas Kitchen Towels

Celebrate the 12 Days of Christmas with an embroidered kitchen towel that is sure to bring smiles. Each towel has a unique design and is embroidered using simple stitches.

- purchased set of kitchen towels
- tracing paper
- transfer paper or pen
- embroidery floss
- embroidery needle
- embroidery hoop (optional)
- rickrack or other trims (optional)
- scissors

1. Enlarge and copy the patterns (page 157). Transfer each pattern to one of the towels, positioning it where desired on the towel.
2. If using an embroidery hoop, position the fabric into the hoop. Referring to the color chart on page 157, embroider each of the designs using 3 strands of floss using desired stitches. Press.
3. Stitch rickrack to the edge of the towels if desired.

12 Days of Christmas
Kitchen Towels

Santa's Little Helpers

Love to do projects with the whole family? Well, grab the kids and get started on creating a Christmas crafting tradition! Pretty cupcake liners take on a new use when they are layered together to create a Fun Cupcake Liner Wreath. Be sure and buy plenty of extra candy when you make a Sweet Candy Garland for your holiday tree. Need a simple gift for that favorite teacher or friend? Wrap up a chocolate bar and decorate it like Santa, Rudolph or even a frosty snowman! Create Happy Clothespin Elves with scraps of felt and round-topped clothespins. Whatever you choose to craft, the time you spend together will make lasting memories!

Fun Cupcake Liner Wreath
Instructions are on page 137.

Fun Cupcake
Liner Wreath

Let the little ones help create sweet little treats to give to their special friends. Candy Wrapped Friends are easy to make using a chocolate bar, wrapping paper, cardstock and pom-poms. Adhesive foam dots make the shapes pop with fun. Try making all three of these fun little friends. . .a happy snowman, Rudolph and, of course, Santa himself!

Candy Wrapped Friends

What fun to present a sweet chocolate bar all wrapped up for Christmas!

- tracing paper
- pencil
- scissors
- one flat chocolate bar for each design
- red, brown and white kraft or wrapping paper
- white, brown, tan, red, black and orange cardstock
- transparent tape
- pencil with new eraser
- black ink stamping pad
- adhesive foam dots such as Pop Dots
- crafts glue
- black and red fine-line markers
- various size pom-poms in red, white and gold

1. Trace the patterns (pages 152–153) and cut out.

2. **For the snowman,** wrap a chocolate bar with white kraft paper. Cut the body shapes from white paper. Cut the hat from black paper and the scarf from red paper. Fringe the ends of the scarf by making short cuts in the paper. Cut the nose from orange paper. Use the eraser end of the pencil to make the eyes, mouth and buttons on the white pieces. Adhere the pieces to the wrapped bar using the adhesive foam dots. Tuck the scarf between the first two white sections. Glue the nose and hat to the head piece. Glue small red pom-poms across the brim of the hat. Let dry.

3. **For the reindeer,** wrap a chocolate bar with brown kraft paper. Cut the head shape from brown paper. Cut the antlers and feet from tan paper. Cut the bow tie from red paper. Use the eraser

Candy
Wrapped
Snowman

Candy Wrapped
Rudolph and Santa

end of the pencil to make the eyes on the head. Use the fine-line black marker to draw a mouth. Adhere the head to the wrapped bar using adhesive foam dots. Glue the bow tie under the head. Glue the antlers at the top of the head. Glue the feet at the bottom. Glue a small pom-pom for the nose and a large pom-pom on the bow tie. Let dry.

4. For Santa, wrap a chocolate bar with red wrapping paper. Cut the face shape from tan paper. Cut the beard and mustache from white paper. Cut the hat from red paper. Cut the belt from black paper. Use the eraser end of the pencil to make the eyes on the face piece. Glue the hat, face, beard and belt to the wrapped bar. Adhere the mustache using adhesive foam dots. Draw a mouth using the red fine-line marker. Glue small gold pom-poms on the black belt for a buckle. Glue a white pom-pom at the top of the hat. Let dry.

Little Drummer Boy Drums

Celebrate the music of Christmas by making and decorating little drums for your holiday tree.

- purchased round drum-shaped cardboard form (available at crafts stores)
- acrylic paints in desired colors
- paintbrush
- trims such as ribbon, rickrack, buttons, paper tape, small jingle bells and pom-poms
- tan air-dry clay (for drumsticks)
- wood skewers (for drumsticks)
- crafts glue
- scissors
- hot-glue gun and glue sticks

1. Remove the lid from the cardboard drum shape and paint both the drum bottom and top using acrylic paint. Let dry.

2. Plan the design on the drum. Glue the trims on the drums using crafts glue or hot glue. Let dry. Add a ribbon or rickrack for hanging.

3. To make the drumsticks, cut the skewer to about 3". Form a ball using the clay and poke the skewer into the clay ball. Let dry. Glue to the top of the drum.

Little Drummer Boy Drums

Happy Clothespin Elves

Let the kids choose the colors and trims for the Little Drummer Boy Drums and the Happy Clothespin Elves. And of course they'll love choosing the candy for a magical Sweet Candy Garland!

Sweet Candy Garland

Happy Clothespin Elves

Make time in your busy holiday schedule to craft ornaments with your children and grandchildren. You'll be rewarded with heirlooms to enjoy every Christmas!

- wooden clothespins
- felt, such as National Nonwovens: dark and light green, red and peach, dark and light blue or desired colors
- sequins
- tiny small pom-poms: red, green and white (for hats)
- white pom-pom (for hair)
- black acrylic paint
- paintbrush
- chenille stems in colors to match felt clothes
- 1/2" wood beads (for hands)
- hot-glue gun and glue sticks
- scissors

(continued on page 138)

Sweet Candy Garland
Instructions are on page 138.

Color-Etched Greeting Cards

Let the little ones show their creativity by etching designs into an almost magical card of colors!

- white cardstock
- crayons
- black acrylic paint
- paintbrush
- etching tool such as a pointed wooden stick or coin
- colored pre-folded greeting cards

1. Choose the desired size of cardstock to be used that fits the front of the pre-folded cards. Using crayons, color in multiple colors on the cardstock, covering the entire paper in random fashion.

2. Paint over the crayon using black acrylic paint. Paint two coats if needed. Let the paint dry.

3. Use the etching tool to scratch a design through the paint revealing the colors underneath. Dust away any black paint pieces.

4. Adhere the cardstock to the front of the folded greeting card.

Color-Etched Greeting Cards

Color-Etched Greeting Cards feature the work of young artists and can be saved and framed later. Handprint and Fingerprint Hot Pads capture a moment in time and make great gifts for special family members.

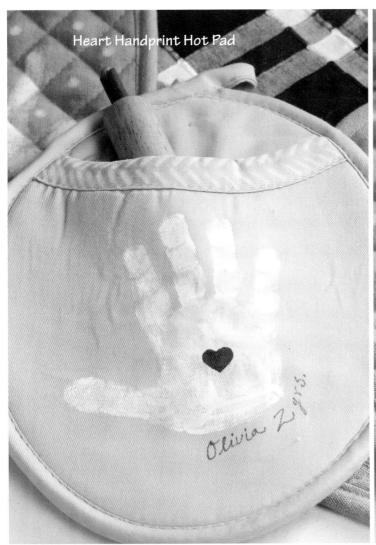

Heart Handprint Hot Pad

Olivia 2 yrs.

Lacy Handprint Hot Pad

Olivia 2 yrs.

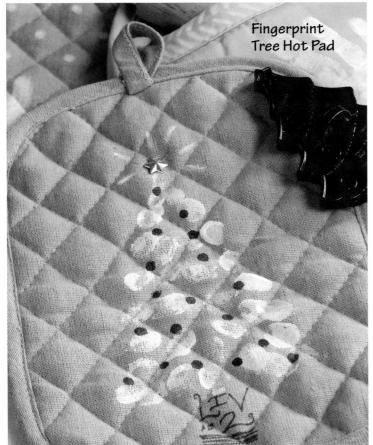

Fingerprint Tree Hot Pad

Handprint Hot Pads

Grandpa and Grandma will love these hot pads printed with the little one's own handprints and fingerprints.

- purchased hot pads
- waxed paper
- fabric paint
- paintbrush
- fine-line permanent marker
- lace or fabric trims; buttons
- fabric glue

1. Wash and iron the hot pads. If there is a pocket on the hot pad, slip a piece of waxed paper into the pocket. Using a brush, paint the white paint on the child's hand or finger. Press the hand or finger onto the hot pad making the desired design. Wash child's hand. Let the hot pad dry. Remove waxed paper.
2. Add details to the hot pad using permanent markers including the name and age of the child. Add fabric or button trims using fabric glue if desired.

Wrapped-Up GIFTS from the KITCHEN

Stir up some holiday goodies and package them as clever gifts to share with those special people on your holiday list. Try swirling together some Christmas Cookie Pops for the kids next door or filling jars plum full of Plum Jam for that always-there-to-help friend. Need a quick gift for that new teacher? Little hands would love to present a box of homemade candy or a gingerbread man cutout cookie in a sweet parchment envelope. Everyone loves bar cookies, so decorate a pretty box and fill it with yummy holiday bars to give to a valued coworker or friend. A basket of Christmas Croissants is always a welcome gift. . .add a jar of local honey to make the gift complete. No matter what you choose to make and give, these homemade goodies, all wrapped up for Christmas, will be favorite gifts of the season!

Christmas Cookie Pops

So pretty to look at and lovely to share, cookie pops are a holiday favorite!

½ c. butter, softened
½ c. shortening
1 c. sugar
1 c. powdered sugar
2 eggs, beaten
¾ c. oil
2 t. vanilla extract
4 c. all-purpose flour
1 t. baking soda
1 t. salt
1 t. cream of tartar
Lollipop sticks
Garnish: frosting

Beat butter and shortening until fluffy; add sugars, beating well. Beat in eggs, oil and vanilla. In a separate bowl, combine flour and remaining ingredients. Cover and chill 2 hours. Shape dough into $1^1/_2$" balls. Place 2 inches apart on ungreased baking sheets. Insert a stick about one inch into each ball. Flatten slightly. Bake at 350 degrees for 10 to 11 minutes, until set. Let cool 2 minutes on baking sheets; cool completely on wire racks. Frost with Best-Ever Bakery Frosting (page 90). To make swirls, tint half the frosting red. Place red and white frosting in decorating bag with extra large tip. Pipe swirl on each cookie. Makes $4^1/_2$ dozen.

Claire Bertram
Lexington, Ky

Christmas Cookie Pops
Swirl Cookie Pop Bag

Swirl Cookie Pop Bag
Instructions are on page 138.

Christmas Fruit Bars

These bar cookies have been one of my favorites since I was a kid. They're easy to make and very pretty too!

½ c. shortening
1 ⅓ c. brown sugar, packed
½ t. cinnamon
¼ t. ground cloves
¼ t. nutmeg
2 eggs
1 ½ c. all-purpose flour
1 t. salt
½ t. baking soda
2 c. candied fruit, chopped
1 c. chopped nuts

Blend together shortening, brown sugar and spices until fluffy. Stir in eggs; set aside. Sift together flour, salt and baking soda; add to shortening mixture. Spread evenly in a greased 13"x9" baking pan; sprinkle fruit and nuts evenly over top. Bake at 350 degrees for 25 minutes. Cut into bars. Makes 2½ to 3 dozen.

Dana Irish
Pflugerville, TX

Christmas Fruit Bars

Quick & Easy Lemon Bars

Simple to make…a holiday must-have.

16-oz. pkg. one-step angel food
    cake mix
22-oz. can lemon pie filling
Optional: chopped pecans, flaked
    oconut

Mix dry cake mix and pie filling in a large bowl. Spread in a greased 15"x10" jelly-roll pan; top with pecans or coconut as desired. Bake at 350 degrees for 30 minutes. Let cool; cut into bars. Makes 2½ dozen.

Lynda McCormick
Burkburnett, TX

Quick & Easy Lemon Bars

Pack up a pretty box filled with Christmas Fruit Bars, Quick & Easy Lemon Bars and Minty Cheesecake Bars. What a quick and special gift!

Minty Cheesecake Bars

4 1-oz. sqs. unsweeted baking
   chocolate, coarsely chopped
½ c. plus 2 T. butter, divided
2 c. sugar
4 eggs, divided
2 t. vanilla extract
1 c. all-purpose flour
8-oz. pkg. cream cheese,
   softened
1 T. cornstarch
14-oz. can sweetened condensed
   milk
1 t. peppermint extract
Optional: green food coloring
1 c. semi-sweet chocolate chips
½ c. whipping cream
Garnish: crushed peppermints

Melt baking chocolate with $\frac{1}{2}$ cup butter; stir until smooth. Combine chocolate mixture with sugar, 3 eggs, vanilla and flour in a large bowl, blending well. Spread in a greased 13"x9" baking pan. Bake for 12 minutes at 350 degrees. Beat together cream cheese, remaining butter and cornstarch in a medium bowl until fluffy. Gradually beat in condensed milk, remaining egg, extract and food coloring, if desired. Pour mixture over hot chocolate layer; bake for 30 minutes, or until set. Combine chocolate chips and cream in a small saucepan. Cook over low heat until smooth, stirring constantly. Spread over mint layer; sprinkle with crushed peppermints and let cool. Refrigerate until set; cut into bars. Store covered in refrigerator. Makes 2 to 3 dozen bars.

Jo Ann

Pretty Cookie Bar Box Instructions start on page 138.

Minty Cheesecake Bars

Pretty Cookie Bar Box

Orangy-Ginger Biscotti

The flavor of this biscotti will keep you coming back for more!

2/3 c. almonds
1 3/4 c. cake flour
2 t. ground ginger
1 t. baking powder
1 c. butter, softened
1 c. brown sugar, packed
6 T. plus 2 t. sugar
2 T. orange zest
2 egg yolks, divided and beaten
½ t. vanilla extract
2/3 c. pistachios, chopped
melted white chocolate

Finely grind almonds, flour, ginger and baking powder in a food processor; set aside. Blend together butter, brown sugar and 6 tablespoons sugar until light and fluffy. Add zest, one egg yolk and vanilla; beat well. Mix in dry ingredients; stir just until blended. Stir in pistachios. Divide dough in half. Using floured hands, roll each half on a lightly floured surface into a 1/2-inch thick log. Arrange logs 4 inches apart on a greased and floured baking sheet. Cover with plastic wrap; refrigerate for one hour. Brush logs with remaining egg yolk; sprinkle with remaining sugar. Bake at 350 degrees for about 30 minutes, until deep golden and firm to touch. Let cool for 10 minutes. Using a serrated knife, cut logs crosswise into 1/2-inch thick slices. Arrange sliced-side down on baking sheet. Bake at 300 degrees until golden on top, about 12 minutes. Turn over; bake until golden, about 12 minutes. Transfer biscotti to a wire rack; cool completely. Drizzle with melted white chocolate if desired. Store in an airtight container at room temperature. Makes 1 1/2 dozen.

Carrie O'Shea
Marina Del Ray, CA

Biscotti Wrap Instructions are on page 139.

Orangy-Ginger Biscotti
Biscotti Wrap

Berry Scones
Berry Scone Mix Jar and Tag

So yummy with a mug of coffee, Orangy-Ginger Biscotti makes a great gift! Berry Scone Mix fits perfectly in a quart jar and makes warm scones in no time!

Instructions for back of tag:
Place scone mix in a large bowl; toss gently to mix. Add one beaten egg and $^1/_4$ cup water; stir just until moistened. Turn dough out onto a lightly floured surface; quickly knead gently for 12 to 15 strokes, or until nearly smooth. Pat to $^1/_2$-inch thick. Cut into desired shapes and place one inch apart on an ungreased baking sheet. Brush with milk. Bake at 400 degrees for 12 to 15 minutes, or until golden. Transfer to a wire rack to cool slightly; serve warm. Makes 6 to 8 scones.

*Brenda Smith
Delaware, OH*

Berry Scone Mix Jar and Tag Instructions are on page 139.

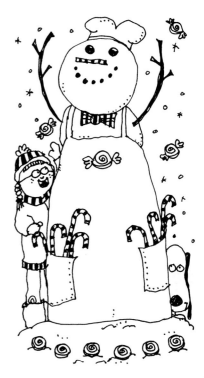

Berry Scone Mix

To make vanilla sugar…simply slice a vanilla bean in half lengthwise and add both halves to $^1/_2$ cup sugar. Let stand for 2 weeks.

2 c. all-purpose flour
½ c. vanilla sugar
¼ c. powdered milk
2 t. baking powder
1 t. lemon zest
¼ t. salt
$^1/_3$ c. shortening
1 c. sweetened, dried blueberries

Stir together flour, sugar, milk, baking powder, lemon zest and salt in a large bowl. Cut in shortening using a pastry cutter or fork, until mixture resembles coarse crumbs. Stir in berries. Pour into a one-quart, wide-mouth canning jar; pack down gently. Add additional berries to fill jar if necessary. Secure lid; attach tag and instructions on back of tag. Store at room temperature for up to 6 weeks, or freeze up to 6 months.

You'll be giving them visions of sugarplums this Christmas when you present your own homemade Plum Jam all wrapped up for the holidays with cupcake-liner toppers. Fill a pretty box with Orange Swirl Fudge and Cool & Creamy Peppermint Fudge for a sweet gift they'll love.

Plum Jam

A jar of homemade jam adds so much to a gift of bread, muffins or scones.

4 lbs. plums, pitted and chopped
6 c. sugar
1$\frac{1}{2}$ c. water
¼ c. lemon juice
4 1-pint jars with lids, sterlized

Combine all ingredients in a saucepan; bring to a boil over medium heat, stirring occasionally until sugar dissolves. Cook rapidly until mixtures coats the back of a spoon, about 20 minutes. As mixture thickens, stir frequently to prevent sticking. Pour into hot sterilized jars, leaving $\frac{1}{4}$-inch headspace. Wipe rims; secure lids with rings. Process in a boiling water bath for 15 minutes. Cool on a towel; check for seals. Makes 4 jars.

Sharon Tillman
Hampton, VA

Festive Jam Jar Instructions are on page 139.

Plum Jam
Festive Jam Jar

Orange Swirl Fudge

I have my own sweet shop, Karen's Konfections, and I love to try new recipes. This recipe is a winner!

3 c. sugar
²/₃ c. whipping cream
³/₄ c. butter
1 1-oz. pkg. white chocolate chips
7-oz. jar marshmallow creme
12 drops yellow food coloring
9 drops red food coloring
1 T. orange extract

In a large saucepan over medium heat, combine sugar, cream and butter. Stir mixture until it reaches the soft-ball stage, or 234 to 243 degrees on a candy thermometer. Remove from heat. Add chocolate chips and marshmallow creme; stir until melted and smooth. Reserve one cup fudge; to the remaining fudge add food coloring and extract, mixing well. Pour into a buttered 13"x9" baking pan. Spoon reserved fudge over top; swirl with a table knife. Cool; cut into squares. Makes about 3 dozen.

Karen Hood Keeney
Bronston, KY

Cool & Creamy Peppermint Fudge

2 10-oz. pkgs. white chocolate
   chips
14-oz. can sweetened condensed
   milk
½ to 1 t. peppermint extract
1 ½ c. peppermint candy canes,
   crushed
¼ t. red or green food coloring
Garnish: crushed peppermint
   candy canes

Combine chocolate chips and condensed milk in a saucepan over medium heat. Stir frequently until chips are almost melted. Remove from heat; continue to stir until smooth. When chips are completely melted, stir in extract, food coloring and crushed candy. Place aluminum foil in a 8"x8" baking pan. Grease foil and spread chocolate mixture over foil. Top with crushed peppermint candy canes. Chill for 2 hours; cut into squares. Makes about 5 dozen.

Vickie

Candy Box Instructions are on page 140.

Orange Swirl
Fudge and
Cool & Creamy
Peppermint Fudge
Candy Box

Bake up a loaf of Cherry & Apple Bread and present it on a cutting board wrapped in a pretty bandanna. What could be better than your own personal gingerbread man? Slide the Orange Gingerbread Cut-Outs each into their own little envelope for giving.

Cherry & Apple Bread

Our family loves to eat quick breads and muffins for breakfast any time of year!

$^1/_2$ c. shortening
1 c. plus 1 T. sugar, divided
2 eggs, beaten
$^1/_2$ c. dried cherries
1 c. apples, peeled, cored and
    finely chopped
$1^1/_2$ T. milk
$^1/_2$ t. vanilla extract
1 c. all-purpose flour
1 t. baking soda
$^1/_2$ t. salt
$1^3/_4$ t. cinnamon, divided
1 c. chopped nuts
Garnish: frosting, coarse sugar

In a large bowl, beat shortening and one cup sugar; add eggs and mix well. Stir in dried cherries, apples, milk and vanilla. In a separate bowl, mix flour, baking soda, salt and $^1/_2$ teaspoon cinnamon; add to shortening mixture, mixing well. Fold in nuts. Spoon into a greased 9"x5" loaf pan. Combine remaining sugar and cinnamon; sprinkle over top. Bake at 350 degrees for 50 minutes to one hour, until a toothpick inserted into center of loaf tests clean. Cool. Drizzle with Powdered Sugar Frosting (page 73) and coarse sugar. Makes one loaf.

Abi Buening
Grand Forks, ND

Holiday Bread Wrap Instructions are on page 140.

Cherry & Apple Bread
Holiday Bread Wrap

Orange Gingerbread Cut-Outs
Gingerbread Man Envelope and Tag

Orange Gingerbread Cut-Outs

Fresh orange zest gives these gingerbread cookies an extra zing! This is one of my favorite cookie recipes from early fall until the end of the holiday season. Make them into sweet little gingerbread men and tuck them into a parchment envelope for the perfect gift!

2$\frac{3}{4}$ c. all-purpose flour
$\frac{1}{2}$ t. baking soda
$\frac{1}{2}$ t. salt
1 t. ground ginger
$\frac{2}{3}$ c. light molasses
$\frac{1}{3}$ c. brown sugar, packed
$\frac{1}{3}$ c. butter, softened
1 egg, beaten
2 t. orange zest
Garnish: frosting, mini candies

In a bowl, mix flour, baking soda, salt and ginger; set aside. In a separate large bowl, combine molasses, brown sugar, butter, egg and orange zest. Beat with an electric mixer on medium speed until smooth and creamy. Add flour mixture; beat on low speed until well mixed. Divide dough into 2 balls. Cover and refrigerate one to 2 hours, until firm. Using one ball of dough at a time, roll out $\frac{1}{4}$-inch thick on a well-floured surface. Cut out with gingerbread man cookie cutters. Place on greased baking sheets, one inch apart. Bake at 375 degrees for 6 to 8 minutes, until cookies spring back when touched. Cool completely on wire racks. Decorate cookies as desired with Powdered Sugar Frosting, and candies. Makes about 4 dozen.

Powdered Sugar Frosting:
4 c. powdered sugar
$\frac{1}{2}$ c. butter, softened
2 t. vanilla extract
3 to 4 T. milk

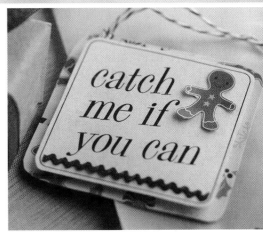

Combine powdered sugar, butter and vanilla in a large bowl. Beat with an electric mixer on low speed, adding milk to desired consistency.

Zoe Bennett
Columbia, SC

Gingerbread Man Envelope and Tag
Instructions are on page 140.

Stained Glass Candy

You can use any flavor of extract or color of food coloring in this easy recipe.

1 c. water
3¹/₂ c. sugar
1¹/₂ c. light corn syrup
1 T. almond extract
food coloring in desired colors

Combine water, sugar and corn syrup in a large heavy saucepan over medium-high heat, stirring constantly. When sugar dissolves, bring to a boil without stirring, until mixture reaches the hard-crack stage, or 290 to 310 degrees on a candy thermometer. Remove from heat. When mixture stops bubbling, stir in extract and coloring. **Note:** to make more than one color of candy, divide mixture and add desired color to each small batch. Spread ¹/₄-inch thick in a greased 18"x12" jelly-roll pan. Cool for 45 minutes in refrigerator. Break into pieces. Makes 2¹/₂ dozen.

Samantha Sparks
Madison, WI

Candy Tag Instructions are on page 141.

Stained Glass Candy
Candy Tag

Peppermint Candy Canes

You'll love this old-fashioned recipe that's sure to bring smiles!

2 c. sugar
½ c. light corn syrup
½ c. water
¼ t. cream of tartar
¾ t. peppermint extract
¾ to 1 t. red food coloring

In a large, heavy saucepan, blend together sugar, corn syrup, water and cream of tartar; stir to dissolve sugar. Cook over medium heat until candy thermometer reaches the hard-ball stage, or 250 to 269 degrees on a candy thermometer. Remove from heat. Add peppermint extract; blend well. Divide into 2 portions. Add coloring to one portion; mix well. Pour candy onto 2 greased plates; let cool. When cool enough to handle, form into 2 ropes; twist white and red candy together. Cut into desired lengths and form into canes. Makes 6.

*Diana Chaney
Olathe, KS*

Candy Cane Box and Tag Instructions are on page 141.

So pretty and bright, Stained Glass Candy is quick to make but looks almost regal! Peppermint Candy Canes taste so sweet and are almost magical to make. Let the kids help you stir up these colorful little treats.

A basket full of Christmas Croissants is a warm & welcome gift for anyone! Fruity Raspberry Vinegar and Rosemary Vinegar are the perfect colors for the holidays. Dress up the bottles with embroidery floss and pretty printed tags.

Christmas Croissants

This recipe is oh-so-easy! It was given to me many years ago...one of the hundreds of recipes I have collected over the years.

2 envs. active dry yeast
1 c. warm water
5 c. all-purpose flour, divided
$\frac{1}{3}$ c. sugar
$1\frac{1}{2}$ t. salt
$\frac{1}{4}$ c. butter, melted and cooled
    slightly
$\frac{3}{4}$ c. evaporated milk
2 eggs, divided
1 c. chilled butter
1 T. water

In a large bowl, dissolve yeast in very warm water, 110 to 115 degrees; let stand 5 minutes. In a separate bowl, combine one cup flour, sugar and salt. Add to yeast mixture; stir. Add melted butter, milk and one egg; beat until smooth. To a separate large bowl, add remaining flour; cut in chilled butter until mixture is crumbly. Add yeast mixture; mix well but do not knead. Cover; refrigerate overnight. Punch down dough. Turn out onto a lightly floured surface. Knead about 6 times and divide into 4 pieces. On a floured surface, roll out each piece into a 16" circle; cut each circle into 8 wedges using a pizza cutter. Roll up wedges beginning at the wide end; place point side-down, 3 inches apart, on ungreased baking sheets. Curve ends to form a crescent. Cover and let rise in a warm place for one hour. Beat remaining egg with water; brush over rolls. Bake at 325 degrees for 20 to 25 minutes, until lightly golden. Makes 32.

Laurie Ellithorpe
Argyle, NY

Croissant Basket and Tag Instructions are on page 141.

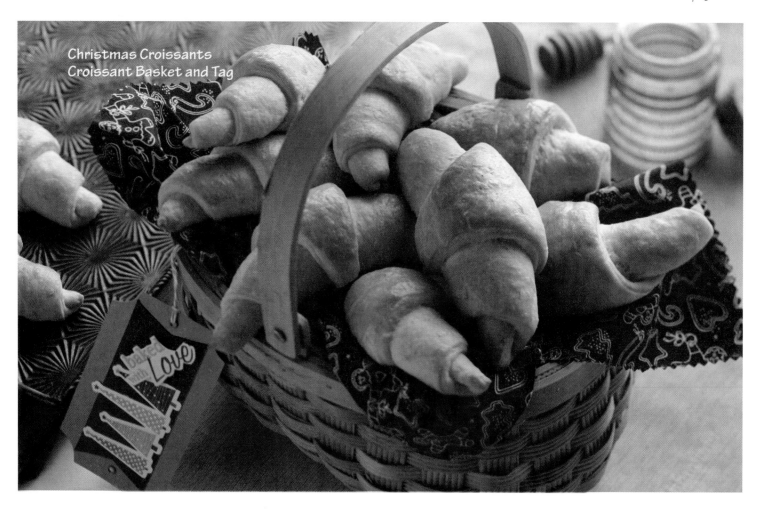

Christmas Croissants
Croissant Basket and Tag

Fruity Raspberry Vinegar

So nice drizzled on fresh berries.

3 c. cider vinegar
1 c. raspberries
2 T. sugar
3 ½-pint bottles and lids,
    sterilized

Combine all ingredients in a medium glass mixing bowl; mix gently. Using a funnel, carefully pour mixture into bottles; cover tightly with lids and store at room temperature. Makes 3 bottles.

Kelly Alderson
Erie, PA

Rosemary Vinegar

Adds a great flavor to steamed veggies.

4 c. white vinegar
$^{2}/_{3}$ c. water
6 sprigs fresh rosemary
4 ½-pint bottles and lids,
    sterilized

Combine vinegar and water in a saucepan over medium-high heat until mixture begins to boil. Remove from heat. Slip 3 sprigs of rosemary into each bottle. Using a funnel, carefully pour the hot vinegar into the bottles. Cover tightly with lids; store at room temperature. Makes 4 bottles.

Anna McMaster
Portland, OR

Vinegar Bottle and Tag Instructions start on page 141.

Fruity Raspberry Vinegar
Rosemary Vinegar
Vinegar Bottles and Tags

We are sure that Santa would love to feed Rudolph some Reindeer Food. . . .but the kids might eat it all first! Give a gift they can make in their own kitchen. Yummy Chocolate Cake Mix fits in a jar and bakes up to make a warm chocolatey cake to enjoy on Christmas Eve.

Reindeer Food

When my youngest son Matthew was 7, he made this snack mix. We give it as Christmas presents to aunts and uncles…everyone loves it!

14-oz. pkg. oat cereal with mini
    marshmallows
10-oz. pkg. tiny pretzels
14-oz. pkg. candy-coated
    chocolate
$3^{1}/_{2}$ c. mixed nuts
16-oz. pkg. white melting
    chocolate, chopped

    Mix together all ingredients except melting chocolate in a large bowl; set aside. Melt white chocolate in a microwave-safe bowl on high setting for one minute, stir, then repeat at 15 second intervals until melted. Pour over dry ingredients; mix well. Spread onto wax paper; let stand for about one hour. Store in an airtight container. Makes 24 cups.

Stephanie Kemp
Millersburg, OH

Mix Wrap and Tag Instructions are on page 142.

Reindeer Food
Mix Wrap and Tag

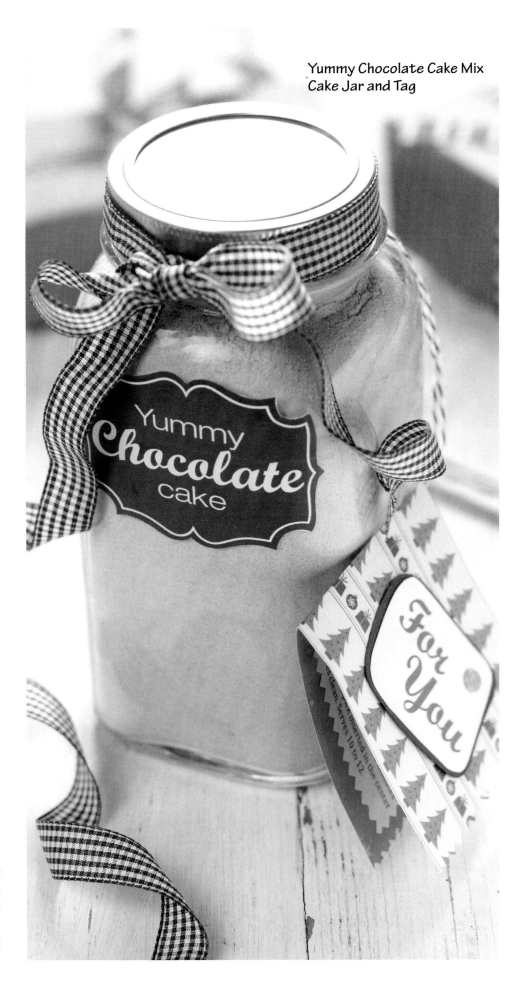

Yummy Chocolate Cake Mix
Cake Jar and Tag

Yummy Chocolate Cake Mix

Everyone loves chocolate cake! This gift and recipe make it easy to have a warm cake right out o f the oven!

3 c. all-purpose flour
2 c. sugar
2 t. baking soda
3 T. baking cocoa
2 t. salt

Sift all ingredients together; pack into a one-quart, wide-mouth jar. Secure lid; fold tag and include instructions inside of the tag.

Instructions for inside of tag:
Place mix in a large mixing bowl; make 3 wells in mixture. Pour one teaspoon vanilla extract into one well, ³/4 cup oil into another and 2 tablespoons white vinegar into the last well. Pour 2 cups cold water on top; mix well. Spread in an ungreased 13"x9" baking pan; bake at 350 degrees for 30 to 40 minutes or until a toothpick inserted in the center removes clean. Serves 10 to 12.

Vickie

Cake Jar and Tag Instructions are on page 142.

COZY Christmas Eve SUPPeR

Gather the family together for a Christmas Eve supper they'll always remember. Soups and casseroles are traditional night-before-Christmas favorites. Try making a Curried Pumpkin Bisque and top it with a drizzle of cream in the shape of a Christmas tree. Or serve Chili with Corn Dumplings. . . it is a hearty meal that they'll all love. Just add a salad and the meal is complete. Try a make-ahead casserole or a simple-to-make chowder. And don't forget the sweets at the end of your cozy supper! Make a batch of Holly Cookies or Holiday Jam Cookies to serve with some Christmas Eve Wassail. Whatever you choose for your cozy dinner, you'll cherish the time you share together on this magical Christmas Eve night.

Curried Pumpkin Bisque

Curried Pumpkin Bisque

My family really enjoys this light soup during the winter. It is my own recipe and makes an excellent first course for a Christmas feast. It is very simple to prepare.

1 onion, chopped
$1/4$ c. butter
2 T. all-purpose flour
$1/2$ t. curry powder
$1/2$ t. garlic salt
$1/8$ t. ground ginger
15-oz. can pumpkin
$14^1/2$-oz. can chicken broth
12-oz. can evaporated milk
Optional: red pepper flakes,
    whipping cream or sour cream

In a skillet over medium heat, sauté onion in butter until onion is translucent. Add flour and seasonings, stirring constantly. Slowly stir in pumpkin and broth; simmer for 2 to 3 minutes. Add evaporated milk; heat until bisque is simmering, but not yet boiling. Garnish individual bowls of soup with a sprinkle of red pepper flakes or a swirl of cream before serving, if desired. Serves 4 to 5.

Joyce Teague
Providence, KY

Best-Ever Italian Bread

Serve this yummy bread with any favorite soup on Christmas Eve.

1 loaf Italian bread
$1/2$ c. grated Parmesan cheese
$1/3$ c. mayonnaise
$1/4$ t. dried basil
$1/4$ t. garlic powder
$1/8$ t. dried oregano
$1/8$ t. garlic salt

Slice loaf into 12 slices without cutting through the bottom. Place on an ungreased baking sheet. Combine remaining ingredients in a small bowl and mix well. Spread mixture between slices and over top of loaf. Bake at 400 degrees until golden, about 12 to 14 minutes. Serves 6.

Denise Mainville
Huber Heights, OH

Chili with Corn Dumplings

Chili with Corn Dumplings has just the right amount of cilantro to make it full of flavor. The corn in the chili adds a sweet surprise, and the dumplings make it a hearty entrée. Sure to become a Christmas Eve tradition, Cheesy Chicken Chowder is loaded with healthy vegetables in a rich cheesy broth.

Chili with Corn Dumplings
So simple yet so satisfying.

1^1/$_2$ lbs. ground beef
¾ c. onion, chopped
15-oz. can corn, divided
16-oz. can stewed tomatoes
16-oz. can tomato sauce
1 t. hot pepper sauce
2 T. chili powder
1 t. garlic, minced
1^1/$_3$ c. biscuit baking mix
^{2}/$_3$ c. cornmeal
^{2}/$_3$ c. milk
3 T. fresh cilantro, chopped

Brown beef and onion in a Dutch oven over medium heat; drain. Set aside ^{1}/$_2$ cup corn; stir remaining corn with liquid, tomatoes, sauces, chili powder and garlic into beef mixture. Heat to boiling. Reduce heat; cover and simmer for 15 minutes. Mix baking mix and cornmeal in a medium bowl; stir in milk, cilantro and reserved corn just until moistened. Drop dough by rounded tablespoonfuls onto simmering chili. Cook over low heat, uncovered, for 15 minutes. Cover and cook an additional 15 to 18 minutes, until dumplings are dry on top. Makes 6 servings.

Tanya Graham
Lawrenceville, GA

Cheesy Chicken Chowder

Warm up after snowman building with a big bowl of this creamy soup.

2 c. chicken broth
2 c. potatoes, peeled and diced
½ c. carrots, peeled and sliced
½ c. celery, sliced
½ c. onion, chopped
½ t. salt
¼ t pepper
¼ c. butter
¼ c. all-purpose flour
2 c. milk
2 c. shredded Cheddar cheese
1 c. cooked chicken, diced
Garnish: shredded cheese

Bring chicken broth to a boil in a stockpot over medium-high heat. Add vegetables, salt and pepper; cover and simmer for 10 minutes. Set aside. Melt butter in a second stockpot over low heat; add flour and mix well. Gradually add milk, stirring constantly until thickened. Add shredded cheese, chicken and broth mixture; heat through without boiling. Garnish with shredded cheese if desired. Makes 6 to 8 servings.

Sue Busse
Marysville, OH

Cheesy Chicken Chowder

Black Cherry Cranberry Salad

I remember my mother making this salad for every Christmas when I was a child. Now, when planning my own holiday meals, this salad is always at the top of the menu!

8-oz. can crushed pineapple
¼ c. water
3-oz. pkg. black cherry
   gelatin mix
16-oz. can whole-berry cranberry
   sauce
1 c. celery, chopped
1 c. chopped walnuts
¼ c. lemon juice

In a saucepan over medium heat, mix undrained pineapple and water. Heat to boiling; add gelatin mix and stir until gelatin is dissolved. Add remaining ingredients and stir well. Transfer to a 6-cup serving dish. Chill in refrigerator for 4 hours, or until firm. Makes 8 servings.

Leigh Ellen Eades
Summersville, WV

Add some freshness to your Christmas Eve supper with Irene's Layered Salad. This classic recipe can be made ahead of time, giving you time to wrap another gift! Seafood Lovers' Lasagna features the same cheese and pasta combination of a classic lasagna with the twist of seafood instead of beef.

Irene's Layered Salad

Your family will love this make-ahead salad so much there won't be any leftovers!

½ c. mayonnaise
1 T. sugar
¼ t. salt
¼ t. pepper
6 c. mixed salad greens
1 red onion, sliced
10-oz. pkg. frozen peas, thawed
8-oz. pkg. sliced Swiss cheese,
    cut into thin strips
1 lb. bacon, crisply cooked and
    crumbled

Combine mayonnaise, sugar, salt and pepper in a small bowl; set aside. In a large salad bowl, layer one-third of the greens and one-third each of mayonnaise mixture, onion, peas and cheese. Repeat layering twice. Cover and refrigerate for at least 2 hours. At serving time, add bacon and toss. Makes 6 to 8 servings.

Irene Robinson
Cincinnati, OH

Irene's Layered Salad

Seafood Lovers' Lasagna

I think this tastes even better if made a day ahead, then reheated so the flavors set in.

32-oz. container ricotta cheese
1 egg, beaten
1 t. Italian seasoning
1 t. garlic, minced
3 6½-oz. cans shrimp, drained
3 6½-oz. cans crabmeat, drained
16-oz. pkg. frozen corn, thawed
16-oz. pkg. shredded mozzarella cheese, divided
2 14½-oz. cans diced tomatoes, divided
2 16-oz. pkgs. no-boil lasagna, uncooked

Combine ricotta cheese, egg, Italian seasoning, garlic, shrimp, crabmeat, corn, one cup mozzarella and one can diced tomatoes with juices; set aside. Place one layer of lasagna strips in a 13"x 9" baking pan that has been coated with non-stick vegetable spray. Spread half the ricotta mixture over lasagna; top with one cup mozzarella and ⅓ cup of remaining diced tomatoes. Repeat layers 2 more times, ending with mozzarella and diced tomatoes. Bake covered at 375 degrees for 30 minutes. Serves 6 to 8.

Lisanne Miller
Brandon, MS

Seafood Lovers' Lasagna

Holly Cookies

Picture-perfect Holly Cookies and Holiday Jam Cookies use the sweetness of jam to make them so special. Share these sweet treats at the end of the meal! Then gather everyone together to celebrate the holidays with a mug of Christmas Eve Wassail.

Holly Cookies
Santa will love these…better leave plenty!

2 c. all-purpose flour
1 c. sugar
¾ t. baking powder
¼ t. salt
1 t. cinnamon
½ c. margarine
1 egg, beaten
¼ c. milk plus 3 T. milk, divided
⅔ c. red plum jam
2 c. powdered sugar
½ t. vanilla extract
green food coloring
red cinnamon candies

Combine flour, sugar, baking powder, salt and cinnamon. Cut in margarine until pieces are the size of peas; set aside. Mix egg and ¼ cup milk; add to flour mixture and stir until moistened. Roll out on a floured surface to ^{1}/8-inch thick. Cut out holly shapes with a cookie cutter; place on ungreased baking sheets. Bake at 375 degrees for 8 to 10 minutes; cool. Spread ^{1}/2 teaspoon jam on the bottom of one cookie; top with another. Repeat with remaining cookies; set aside. Blend powdered sugar, vanilla and enough of remaining milk to make a glaze consistency. Tint glaze light green. Spread over the top of each cookie. Arrange 2 to 3 cinnamon candies on the top of each cookie; allow glaze to dry. Makes about 4 dozen.

Flo Burtnett
Gage, OK

Holiday Jam Cookies

Holiday Jam Cookies

My mother made these cookies as far back as I can remember. Sometimes when we got off the school bus, she would have cookies waiting for us. She always used her homemade wild strawberry jam. I like to use raspberry jam...I've been making them myself for nearly 45 years now!

$1/2$ c. shortening
$1/3$ c. sugar
2 t. vanilla extract
1 egg, beaten
$1 2/3$ c. all-purpose flour
$1 1/2$ t. baking powder
Garnish: strawberry or raspberry
   jam

In a bowl, combine shortening, sugar, vanilla and egg. With an electric mixer on medium speed, beat until creamy. Stir in flour and baking powder. Drop dough by teaspoonfuls onto greased or parchment paper-lined baking sheets, one inch apart. Make a small indentation in the center of each cookie; fill each with $1/2$ to $3/4$ teaspoon jam. Bake at 375 degrees for 10 to 12 minutes, until edges are lightly golden. Makes 2 dozen.

Connie Litfin
Carrollton, TX

Christmas Eve Wassail

2 qts. apple cider
64-oz. can pineapple juice
2 c. orange juice
1 c. lemon juice
3 4-inch cinnamon sticks
1 t. whole cloves
8-oz. pkg. red cinnamon candies

Combine all ingredients in a slow cooker. Cover and cook on high setting for 2 hours, or until heated through and candies are melted. Reduce setting to low. Before serving, strain out cloves. Serves 18 to 20.

Rhonda Lawson
Middletown, IN

Christmas Eve
Wassail

Holiday cupcakes by the Dozen

Little morsels of sweet cake goodness are all wrapped up in pretty papers! Yes, they are cupcakes. . . all unique, yummy and perfect to fit in the palm of your hand! Make the cake white, yellow, chocolate, spice or peanut butter! Whatever you choose, be sure and top it with layers of soft, sweet frosting all dressed up for Christmas. Try Golden Cupcakes decorated as soft green trees or topped with rich chocolate frosting and curls. Peanut butter lovers will reach for Chocolate-Peanut Butter Marble Cupcakes drizzled with chocolate ganache and sprinkled with whole peanuts. Love to work with fondant? Try creating Bow-Topped Chocolate Red Wine Cupcakes. They are just as delicious to look at as they are to eat! Have fun making these little cake treasures. . .your family will love you for it!

Golden Cupcakes with Frosted Tree Tops

With a golden color, these yummy made-from-scratch cupcakes are as versatile as they are yummy!

4 eggs, separated
$2^{7}/_{8}$ c. all-purpose flour
$1^{1}/_{2}$ t. baking powder
$^{1}/_{2}$ t. salt
1 c. butter, softened
2 c. sugar
2 t. vanilla extract
1 c. milk
Best Ever Bakery Frosting
Garnish for trees: colored candies, peppermint sugar, white sugar, white chocolate stars

With an electric mixer on high speed, beat egg whites in a small bowl until stiff peaks form. In a medium bowl, combine flour, baking powder and salt. In a large bowl, beat butter on medium speed of electric mixer; gradually beat in sugar until fluffy. Beat in egg yolks, one at a time, and vanilla. With a wooden spoon, stir flour mixture into butter mixture by thirds, alternating with milk. Fold in egg whites. Pour batter into paper-lined muffin cups, filling cups $^{2}/_{3}$ full. Bake at 350 degrees for 15 minutes, until a toothpick tests clean. Cool. Makes 12 cupcakes.

To make white chocolate stars for top of trees, melt white chocolate in microwave until just melted, about 1 minute. Drizzle a star shape onto parchment paper. Let cool.

To make the frosted tree tops, tint Best-Ever Bakery Frosting green. Pipe on top of cooled cupcakes. Add candies or other decorations. Place cooled white chocolate star at top.

Vickie

Golden Cupcakes with Frosted Tree Tops

Best-Ever Bakery Frosting

We love the taste of this frosting! A lady in Nunda, New York gave me this recipe when we stopped in her little bakery, many years ago.

2 16-oz. pkgs powdered sugar
1 c. shortening
1 t. clear vanilla extract
$^{1}/_{2}$ to $^{3}/_{4}$ c. milk

In a large bowl, mix all ingredients together just until moistened, adding milk as needed. Do not overbeat. Makes about 3 cups.

Renee Shock
Beaver Dams, NY

Merry Mocha Frosting

Once when I was ten, Mom baked her best chocolate cake for a picnic. When I got home from school, I saw the bowl of frosting on the counter. I stuck in my finger to take a taste and before I knew it, the bowl was empty! Mom didn't get mad...but from then on, she always hid the frosting bowl!

1/2 c. butter, softened
1 pasteurized egg yolk
2 T. strong brewed coffee
2 1-oz. sqs. baking chocolate, melted
2 1/2 c. powdered sugar
Garnish: sprinkles, chocolate curls

Beat together butter and egg yolk in a small bowl. Add coffee and melted chocolate; mix well. Gradually add powdered sugar; beat until smooth. Makes about 3 1/2 cups, enough for 12 cupcakes. Spread onto cupcakes and add sprinkles and chocolate curls.

To make chocolate curls, use a vegetable peeler to carefully scrape a fine curl of chocolate from a chocolate candy bar.

Susann Minall-Hunter
Spring Hill, FL

When you find a favorite cupcake recipe you can change it up by the frosting you choose. Make Christmas tree cupcakes using the Golden Cupcake recipe. Then use the same cake recipe and frost with Merry Mocha Frosting.

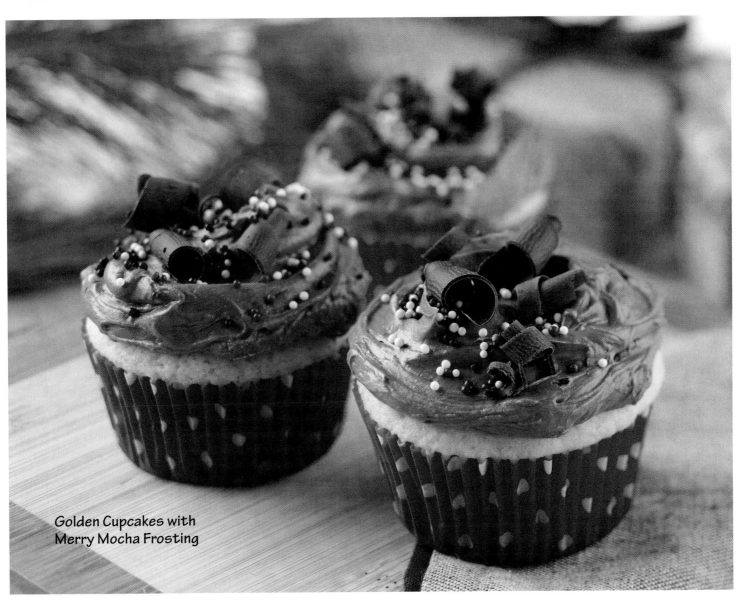

Golden Cupcakes with Merry Mocha Frosting

Pretty Pastel Oatmeal Cupcakes

A rich, dense cupcake hides under the sweet frosting and candies on these Pretty Pastel Oatmeal Cupcakes. Serve them with hot coffee or tea. Oh-so-gooey, Chocolate-Peanut Butter Marble Cupcakes are almost brownie-like and go great with a big glass of milk. Leave a couple for Santa on Christmas Eve!

Pretty Pastel Oatmeal Cupcakes

These cupcakes have just a little spice to make them extra tasty.

1 ^{1}/$_2$ c. boiling water
1 c. quick-cooking oats, uncooked
^{1}/$_2$ c. butter
1 c. sugar
1 c. brown sugar, packed
2 eggs, beaten
1 t. vanilla extract
2 t. cinnamon
^{1}/$_2$ t. nutmeg
1 ^{1}/$_3$ c. all-purpose flour
1 t. baking powder
1 t. baking soda
^{1}/$_2$ t. salt
Cream Cheese Frosting (see
    page 119)

In a medium bowl, pour boiling water over oats; let stand for 20 minutes. In a separate bowl, blend butter and sugars; add to oats. Add eggs, vanilla and spices; beat well and set aside. In a small bowl, mix together remaining ingredients. Add to oat mixture and stir well. Pour batter into paper-lined muffin cups, filling cups ^{2}/$_3$ full. Bake at 350 degrees for 15 to 20 minutes, until cake tests done. Tint Cream Cheese Frosting (page 119) pink and green or leave white. Pipe frosting on top of cupcakes using a large round tip. Decorate with small candies and sugars. Makes 12 cupcakes.

Babette Burgess
Battle Creek, MI

Chocolate-Peanut Butter Marble Cupcakes

I baked these cupcakes for my son because he's fond of both peanut butter and chocolate. When I combined them just for fun, the cupcakes came out very well...warm and yummy!

1 c. all-purpose flour
1 c. sugar
1 t. baking powder
½ t. salt
1 c. semi-sweet chocolate chips, melted and cooled slightly
½ c. butter
5 T. canola oil
2 eggs, beaten
1 t. vanilla extract
1 c. peanut butter chips, melted
Peanut Butter Frosting
Chocolate Ganache
Garnish: dry roasted peanuts

Chocolate-Peanut Butter Marble Cupcakes

In a large bowl, mix flour, sugar, baking powder and salt; set aside. In a separate bowl, combine melted chocolate chips, butter, oil, eggs and vanilla; beat together. Add chocolate mixture to flour mixture. With an electric mixer on medium speed, beat for 3 minutes. Pour batter into paper-lined muffin cups, filling cups ⅔ full. Add small spoonfuls of melted peanut butter chips on top of batter; swirl through batter with a skewer or toothpick. Bake at 350 degrees for 10 to 15 minutes, or until a toothpick inserted in center tests clean. Pipe cupcakes with Peanut Butter Frosting.

To make Chocolate Ganache, heat ½ cup whipping cream until hot (do not boil) and pour cream over ½ cup chocolate chips. Let stand for 15 minutes stirring occasionally until shiny and smooth. Drizzle over cupcakes. Sprinkle with dry roasted peanuts. Makes 12 cupcakes.

Peanut Butter Frosting

16-oz. pkg powdered sugar
½ c. butter
¼ c. milk
¼ c. smooth peanut butter

In a large bowl, mix all ingredients together just until moistened, adding milk as needed. Do not overbeat. Makes about 1½ cups.

Aqsa Masood
Ontario, Canada

White Chocolate Buttercream Frosting

5 1-oz. sqs. white baking chocolate, chopped
¾ c. cream cheese, softened
¼ c. butter, softened
⅛ t. salt
1 t. vanilla extract
2½ c. powdered sugar, divided

Melt chocolate in a double boiler. Remove from heat; set aside until lukewarm. In a large bowl with an electric mixer on medium speed, beat cream cheese and butter until smooth. Add chocolate, salt and vanilla; mix well. Add 2 cups powdered sugar; beat on high speed for 3 minutes. If mixture is too thin, add remaining powdered sugar; beat on high speed for 7 minutes more.

Bow-Topped Chocolate Red Wine Cupcakes

I teach a gourmet cupcake baking class at a local cooking school. This recipe is one of the most popular in the class. My son, who is a professional chef, said these were the best cupcakes he's ever tasted! Topped with fondant bows, they are the prettiest too!

3/4 c. semi-sweet chocolate chips
1/2 c. baking cocoa
1/2 c. boiling water
1 c. butter, softened
1 1/2 c. sugar
4 eggs
1 1/4 c. all-purpose flour
1 1/2 t. baking powder
1 t. salt
3/4 c. Italian sparkling red wine
Powdered Sugar Icing
Garnish: fondant bows

In a bowl, combine chocolate chips and cocoa. Pour boiling water over top and whisk until chocolate is melted. In a large bowl, beat butter and sugar until fluffy. Beat in eggs, one at a time. In a separate bowl, combine flour, baking powder and salt. Slowly add to butter mixture; mix well. Alternately add chocolate mixture and wine to butter mixture; blend well. Pour batter into paper-lined muffin cups, filling cups 2/3 full. Bake at 350 degrees for 15 to 20 minutes, or until a toothpick inserted in the center tests clean. Cool. Frost with Powdered Sugar Icing. Top with White Chocolate Fondant Bows. Makes 18 cupcakes.

Donna Nowicki
Center City, MN

Powdered Sugar Icing

1/4 c. butter, melted
2 1/2 c. powdered sugar
1 t. vanilla extract
2 T. cream cheese, softened
1 to 2 T. milk

Mix all ingredients in a bowl and beat until smooth, adding milk as needed.

White Chocolate Fondant Bows

Melt 12 oz. white candy coating discs. Stir in 1/3 c. corn syrup. Wrap in plastic wrap. Let stand until firm, chilling if necessary. To make bows, knead in red food coloring. Roll on powdered sugar covered surface to 1/8-inch thickness. Cut into 1-inch wide strips. Shape into bows.

Bow-Topped Chocolate Red Wine Cupcakes

Holly-Topped
White Cupcakes

Holly-Topped White Cupcakes

My mom used to bake these delightful made-from-scratch white cupcakes for our family. The chocolate frosting makes them extra special!

4 eggs, beaten
2 c. sugar
2 c. all-purpose flour
2 t. baking powder
$^1/_4$ t. salt
1 t. vanilla extract
$^1/_2$ c. butter
1 c. milk
Best-Ever Bakery Frosting
Garnish: red candies

In a large bowl, beat together eggs and sugar. Add flour, baking powder, salt and vanilla; mix well and set aside. In a saucepan over medium heat, combine butter and milk. Bring to a boil; cool slightly and add to batter. Mix well. Pour batter into paper-lined muffin cups, filling cups $^2/_3$ full. Bake at 350 degrees for 15 to 20 minutes, until cake tests done. Cool; frost with Bitter Chocolate Frosting. To make holly decoration, pipe green tinted Best-Ever Bakery Frosting (page 90) in holly shapes on chocolate frosted cupcakes. Add three red candies for berries. Makes 24 cupcakes.

Bitter Chocolate Frosting

5 1-oz. sqs. unsweetened baking
   chocolate
1 T. butter, softened
1 t. vanilla extract
$1^1/_2$ to $1^3/_4$ c. powdered sugar
3 to 5 T. whipping cream

Melt chocolate in a double boiler over medium heat. Remove from heat; gradually stir in butter and vanilla. With an electric mixer on low speed, beat in powdered sugar and cream to desired consistency.

*Karen Dean
New Market, MD*

Make plenty of Bow-Topped Chocolate Red Wine Cupcakes and Holly-Topped White Cupcakes. That way you'll have some for your family to enjoy and some to give as gifts!

Dinner At GRANDMA'S!

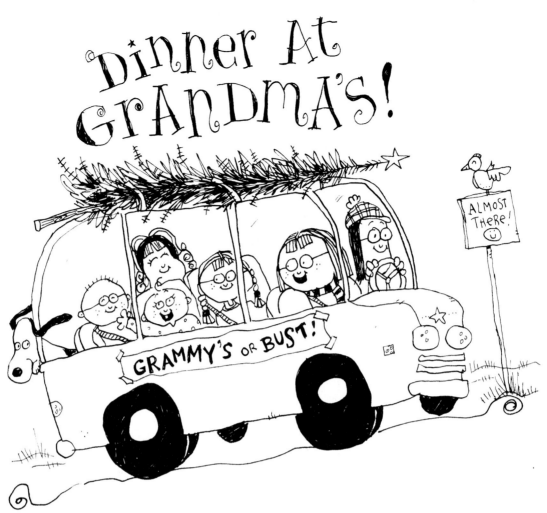

Over the river and through the woods. . .there is nothing better than going to Grandma's house for Christmas dinner! As you step into the house, the aroma tells the tale of the love that went into preparing the special meal for the happiest of days. Start off your holiday feast by cooking an Herbed Roast Turkey Breast in your slow cooker. (That will give you plenty of time for hugs!) Or try easy-to-make Honeyed Raspberry Pork Chops with a honey-mustard sauce. Serve Grandma's Holiday Stuffing, Crunchy Hasselback Potatoes, Sunshine Carrots and Easy Baked Corn for the sides, and be sure to add a fresh tomato or fruit salad to complement the entrée. For dessert, bake a Lemon Upside-Down Cake in a cast iron skillet. Make the day one they will remember with recipes that are sure to please.

Herbed Roast Turkey Breast

Herbed Roast Turkey Breast
This is too good to serve only once or twice a year!

4 to 5-lb. turkey breast
¼ c. fresh parsley, chopped
1 T. fresh thyme or rosemary, chopped
zest and juice of 1 lemon
2 tart apples, cored, peeled and chopped
2 stalks celery, cut in thirds
4 shallots, coarsely chopped
1 c. chicken broth
½ c. dry white wine or chicken broth
2 T. butter, softened
2 T. all-purpose flour

With your fingers, separate skin from turkey breast to make a pocket. Combine herbs and lemon zest; rub under skin. Pat skin back into place. Place apples, celery, shallots, broth and wine or broth in a slow cooker. Place turkey skin-side up on top; drizzle lemon juice over turkey. Cover and cook on low setting for 8 to 10 hours, or on high setting for $3^{1}/2$ to 4 hours, until tender. Remove turkey; if desired, place in a preheated 450 degree oven for 5 to 10 minutes, until skin is golden. Transfer turkey to a serving platter and keep warm. Discard apples and celery; pour drippings into a skillet over medium heat. In a small bowl, combine butter and flour. Whisk into drippings; cook and stir until thickened and bubbly, about 15 minutes. Serve warm gravy with sliced turkey. Serves 4 to 6.

Robin Lakin
LaPalma, CA

So moist and tasty, Grandma's Holiday Stuffing is a must-have addition to Christmas dinner. Add color as well as wonderful flavor with Sunshine Carrots. Just a little orange juice and ginger gives the carrots a sweet and citrus-like tang.

Grandma's Holiday Stuffing
Apples make this stuffing moist and yummy.

1 large loaf day-old bread, torn
Optional: day-old corn muffins, broken up
½ c. butter
1 onion, diced
3 stalks celery diced
Optional: ½ c. sliced mushrooms
2 tart apples, cored and diced
½ c. walnuts, coarsely chopped
½ c. raisins
½ to ¾ c. water
½ to 1 T. poultry seasoning
dried parsley to taste
salt and pepper to taste

Place torn bread in a large baking dish; mix in muffins, if using. Bake at 250 degrees for about 30 minutes, until dried out. Set aside. Melt butter over low heat in a large skillet; sauté onion, celery and mushrooms, if using, until tender. Add apples, walnuts and raisins; stir to coat with butter. Mix in water and seasonings; pour over bread and toss to moisten. Add a little more water if bread is very dry. Use to stuff a 12 to 15-pound turkey before roasting; do not overstuff. Or spread stuffing in a lightly greased 9"x5" baking pan and bake at 350 degrees for 30 to 40 minutes. Serves 8 to 10.

Wendy Lee Paffenroth
Pine Island, NY

Grandma's Holiday Stuffing

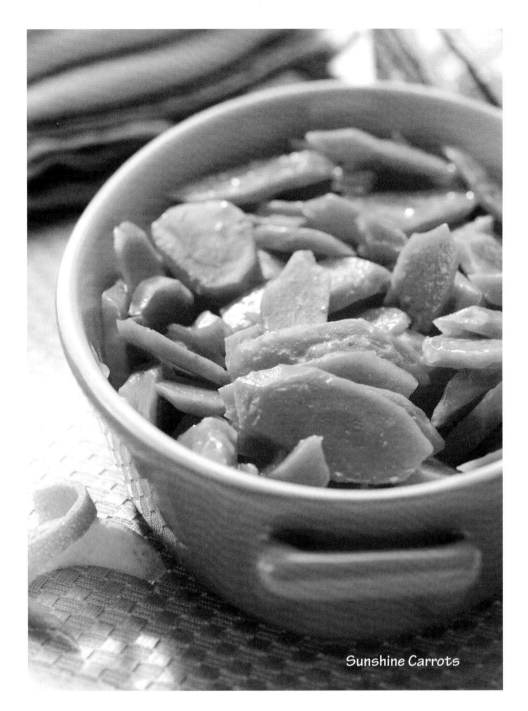

Sunshine Carrots

Belle's Yeast Rolls

Everyone looks forward to my homemade yeast rolls every Christmas. I always add a special touch...a pat of butter nestled in each one.

2 envs. active dry yeast
3 c. warm water
²/₃ c. sugar
2 eggs, beaten
1 T. salt
1 c. shortening, melted
8 to 9 c. all-purpose flour

In a large bowl, dissolve yeast in very warm water, about 110 to 115 degrees; add remaining ingredients. Mix well. Let stand until dough doubles in bulk, at least one hour. Knead dough for about 5 minutes, or until no longer sticky. On a lightly floured surface, roll out dough ¼-inch thick; cut into 20 squares. Place on ungreased baking sheets; allow to rise again, at least one hour. Bake at 450 degrees for 10 to 15 minutes, until golden. Makes 20.

Belle Perry
Lawrenceburg, KY

Sunshine Carrots

A serving of these citrusy carrots will brighten up the frostiest winter day!

5 carrots, peeled
1 T. sugar
1 t. cornstarch
¼ t. salt
¼ t. ground ginger
¼ c. orange juice
2 T. margarine

Cook carrots and set aside. Combine sugar, cornstarch, salt and ginger in a small saucepan over medium heat. Add orange juice, stirring constantly until thickened, about one minute. Stir in margarine. Pour over carrots. Serves 4.

Esther Elian
Skowhegan, ME

Crunchy Hasselback Potatoes

Guests will love these savory baked potatoes, and the fanned-out slices are so pretty on the dinner plate.

8 baking potatoes
3 T. olive oil, divided
$\frac{1}{4}$ c. grated Parmesan cheese
$\frac{1}{2}$ c. soft bread crumbs
1 t. garlic salt
salt to taste
Garnish: chives, sour cream,
    shredded Cheddar cheese,
    bacon bits

With a sharp knife, slice each potato several times from side to side, about $\frac{1}{4}$-inch apart, not quite through to the bottom. Place potatoes on a lightly greased baking sheet. Brush potatoes with 2 tablespoons oil. Mix together remaining oil and other ingredients except garnish. Spoon mixture evenly over potatoes; gently pat mixture between potato slices. Cover with aluminum foil. Bake at 400 degrees for 35 minutes. Uncover; bake an additional 20 minutes. Add toppings as desired. Makes 8 servings.

Heidi Fontes
Brighton, CO

Crunchy Hasselback Potatoes

Cheesy Scalloped Potatoes

These potatoes are easy to make and look so pretty on a serving plate.

$\frac{1}{4}$ c. butter
$\frac{1}{4}$ c. all-purpose flour
2 c. milk
8-oz. pkg. shredded sharp
    Cheddar cheese
1 t. salt
$\frac{1}{4}$ t. pepper
5 potatoes, peeled and sliced
2 onions, sliced

Melt butter in a saucepan over low heat; blend in flour and cook for one minute. Whisk in milk. Cook, stirring constantly, until slightly thickened. Stir in cheese until melted. Add salt and pepper. Spread half of sauce in the bottom of a greased 13"x9" glass baking pan. Arrange potatoes and onions over sauce; top with remaining sauce. Bake, uncovered, at 350 degrees for about one hour, until potatoes are tender. Makes 8 servings.

Debbie Osborn
Westerville, OH

Easy Baked Corn

Mix together all fruits; stir in cider and lemon juice. Chill for 2 to 3 hours. Drain, reserving juice. Combine mayonnaise and 1/3 cup reserved fruit juice. Arrange fruit on lettuce leaves; drizzle with mayonnaise mixture. Serves 6.

Leah Caplan
Fairfax, VA

Creamy Broccoli Casserole

Perfect for busy holidays…just pop this dish in the oven and wrap some gifts while it's baking!

2 10-oz. pkgs. frozen broccoli, thawed and drained
2 10-oz. pkgs. frozen spinach, thawed and drained
10 3/4 oz. can cream of mushroom soup
10 3/4 oz. can cream of celery soup
6-oz. can French fried onions, divided
½ c. shredded Cheddar cheese

Combine first 4 ingredients in a large bowl; stir in half the French fried onions. Pour into an ungreased 13"x9" baking pan; sprinkle with remaining onions and cheese. Bake at 350 degrees for 30 to 45 minutes. Serves 8-10.

Patti Rafferty
Levittown, PA

Easy Baked Corn

Yummy and easy! Garnish with slices of red and green pepper to make it festive!

2 c. frozen corn, thawed
2 eggs, beaten
1/4 c. butter, sliced
3/4 c. milk
3 T. sugar
2 T. all-purpose flour
1/4 t. salt
Optional: sliced red and green pepper

Place all ingredients in a blender or food processor; process to a slightly chunky consistency. Pour into a greased 2-quart casserole dish. Bake, uncovered, at 375 degrees for 45 minutes. Makes 6 servings.

Susan Maher
Arnold, MD

Winter Fruit Salad

This refreshing salad makes a wonderful addition to any holiday dinner. Let the children help prepare this easy salad that the entire family will enjoy!

2 oranges, peeled and sectioned
1 grapefruit, peeled and sectioned
2 apples, peeled, cored and diced
2 pears, peeled, cored and diced
2 bananas, sliced
1 c. purple seedless grapes
1 c. apple cider
1 T. lemon juice
1 1/2 c. mayonnaise
6 lettuce leaves

Crunchy Hasselback Potatoes become little works of art as they are arranged on a serving tray. The Parmesan cheese gives them extra flavor and texture. Everyone looks forward to Easy Baked Corn for the holidays. This recipe is sure to be a favorite!

Chopped Tomato Salad

Add some freshness to your holiday meal with Chopped Tomato Salad. Quick to make Italian Zucchini Bake is a great combination with Honeyed Raspberry Pork Chops. The secret to the sauce is the raspberry jam!

Chopped Tomato Salad

One evening while I was making dinner, my youngest son asked if he could add Kalamata olives to our usual salad, and it grew from there! The dressing is delicious on lots of other salads too.

4 tomatoes, chopped
1 red onion, thinly sliced
1 English cucumber, sliced and
    chopped
$1/2$ c. Kalamata olives, pitted and
    halved
$1/3$ c. fresh basil, shredded
Garnish: crumbled feta cheese

In a large salad bowl, combine all ingredients except feta cheese. Drizzle with Vinaigrette Dressing; toss to coat. Cover and refrigerate at least one hour, tossing once, until flavors are well blended. At serving time, sprinkle with cheese. Serves 4 to 6.

Vinaigrette Dressing:
5 T. red wine vinegar
4 t. olive oil
2 t. Dijon mustard
$1/2$ t. salt
$1/2$ t. pepper

Whisk together ingredients in a small bowl.

Laurel Liebrecht
Yakima, WA

Italian Zucchini Bake

Italian Zucchini Bake

This colorful casserole bakes up with the tastiest melted mozzarella topping.

2 T. butter
1 to 2 zucchini, chopped
1 onion, chopped
4 tomatoes, chopped
1 green pepper, chopped
Italian seasoning to taste
8-oz. pkg. shredded mozzarella
    cheese

Melt butter in a skillet over medium heat. Add zucchini and onion; cook for 5 minutes, until onion is golden. Spoon zucchini mixture into a lightly greased 2-quart casserole dish; stir in tomatoes, green pepper and seasoning. Top with cheese. Bake at 350 degrees for 25 minutes, or until cheese is melted. Serves 4.

Angie Venable
Delaware, Ohio

Honeyed Raspberry Pork Chops

Raspberry jam is the secret to the sauce!

4 boneless pork chops
2 T. all-purpose flour
$1/3$ c. honey mustard
¼ c. raspberry jam
2 T. cider vinegar
1 T. olive oil
1 T. fresh parsley, chopped
Garnish: fresh raspberries

Dredge pork chops in flour, shaking off any excess. In a small bowl, combine honey mustard, jam and vinegar; set aside. Heat oil in a large skillet over medium heat. Add pork chops and sauté until golden on both sides. Stir in mustard mixture; bring to a boil. Reduce heat and simmer for 10 minutes. Sprinkle with parsley. Garnish with fresh raspberries. Serves 4.

Elaine Slabinski
Monroe Township, NJ

Honeyed Raspberry
Pork Chops

Honeyed Mango Salad

So pretty to look at and so yummy to eat, Honeyed Mango Salad adds a touch of color and natural sweetness to your holiday table. Baked in a cast iron frying pan, Lemon Upside-Down Cake is a pretty and tasty dessert for such a special occasion.

Honeyed Mango Salad

We love this simple fruit-filled salad...it's yummy, quick & easy.

2 mangoes, peeled, pitted and
    sliced
2 oranges, segmented
1 banana, sliced
juice of 1 lime
2 T. honey
1/4 c. oil
1/8 t. salt
Garnish: 6 lettuce leaves,
    6 maraschino cherries

Combine fruit and lemon juice in a large bowl; toss to coat. Cover and chill until serving time. Blend lime juice and honey in a small bowl; stir in oil and salt. Drizzle honey mixture over fruit mixture; stir gently. To serve, place lettuce leaves in individual salad bowls; fill with fruit mixture. Top with cherries and any fruit juice remaining in bowl. Serves 6.

Phyl Broich Wessling
Garner, IA

Lemon Upside-Down Cake

Lemon Upside-Down Cake

My mother-in-law always brings us a box of fresh Meyer lemons when she comes from California for the holidays. This is one of my favorite ways to enjoy them!

$3/4$ c. butter, softened and divided
$3/4$ c. plus 2 T. brown sugar, packed
2 Meyer lemons, unpeeled, thinly sliced and seeds removed
$1 1/2$ c. all-purpose flour
2 t. baking powder
$1/4$ t. salt
1 c. sugar
1 t. vanilla extract
2 eggs, separated
$3/4$ c. milk
$1/4$ t. cream of tartar
Optional: whipped topping

Melt $1/4$ cup butter in a 9-inch cast-iron skillet over medium heat. Stir in brown sugar until dissolved; remove from heat. Arrange lemon slices in skillet over brown sugar mixture; set aside. In a bowl, mix flour, baking powder and salt. In a separate large bowl, with an electric mixer on low speed, beat remaining butter and sugar until fluffy. Beat in vanilla and egg yolks, one at a time. Beat in flour mixture alternately with milk; set aside. In a separate bowl, with an electric mixer on high speed, beat egg whites and cream of tartar until stiff peaks form. Fold egg white mixture into batter. Spoon batter into skillet. Bake at 350 degrees for 30 minutes, or until a toothpick inserted in center tests clean. Let cake cool in skillet 15 minutes. Top skillet with a cake plate and turn cake out of skillet. Serve warm or at room temperature; garnish with whipped topping, if desired. Serves 8.

Tiffany Brinkley
Broomfield, CO

Bake up a batch of homemade bread and muffins for the holidays and watch the smiles! Make some Easy Oatmeal Rolls to serve with a hearty soup, or stir up some Southern Hushpuppies to dip in a favorite sauce. Abigail's Crusty White Bread is just as yummy toasted with butter and jam as it is fresh from the oven. Remember having cinnamon rolls on Christmas morning? Try your hand at baking some Buttermilk Cinnamon Rolls for your family this year. Cranberry Upside-Down Muffins are simply delicious and so full of color and flavor. Want something different for your holiday party? Party Bubble Bread is a quick recipe that uses refrigerated biscuits. No matter which bread you choose to try, you'll feel all warm and toasty as you share these good-for-you recipes this holiday season.

Easy Oatmeal Rolls

Easy Oatmeal Rolls

This is an often-requested recipe! I put the dough ingredients in my bread machine and let the machine do the work, but this version calls for doing it by hand. Either way, it's easy and yummy.

1 T. active dry yeast
1 c. warm water
$1/4$ c. sugar
$1^1/2$ t. salt
$1/2$ c. quick-cooking oats or old-
    fashioned oats, uncooked
1 egg, beaten
3 T. oil
3 c. bread flour, divided
Garnish: 1 to 2 T. butter

In a large bowl, dissolve yeast in very warm water, about 110 to 115 degrees. Add sugar, salt, oats, egg, oil and $2^1/4$ cups flour; mix well. Turn onto a lightly floured surface; knead in remaining flour for several minutes. Return dough to bowl; let rise in a warm place for one to $1^1/2$ hours. Punch down; divide and shape dough into golfball-sized balls. Arrange in a greased 13"x9" baking pan. Cover; let rise about one hour. Bake at 350 degrees for 20 to 25 minutes. While rolls are still warm, spread butter over tops. Makes 15 to 18.

Nancy Girard
Chesapeake, VA

Abigail's Crusty White Bread

My mother baked this delightful bread and we enjoyed it hot from the oven with fresh butter and strawberry jam. Now I bake it for my own children as often as I can!

2 $\frac{1}{2}$ c. water
1 T. active dry yeast
1 T. sugar
1 T. salt
7 c. all-purpose flour, divided
$\frac{1}{4}$ to $\frac{1}{2}$ c. butter, softened and
    divided

Heat water until very warm, about 110 to 115 degrees. In a large bowl, combine ½ cup warm water, yeast and sugar. Stir until foamy; let stand for 5 minutes. Add remaining water, salt and 3½ cups flour. Blend with an electric mixer on low speed, using a dough hook if available. Add remaining flour, ¼ cup at a time. Beat on medium speed for 10 minutes, until dough is smooth and elastic. Beat in butter, one tablespoon at a time. Place dough in a lightly greased bowl, turning to coat. Cover with a tea towel; set in a warm place. Let rise for 45 minutes, until double in bulk. Punch down dough and turn out onto a floured surface; divide in half. Roll out each half into a 12-inch by 9-inch rectangle. Fold each rectangle into thirds, pinching seam closed. Place loaves in 2 greased 9"x 5" loaf pans, seam-side down. Cover again and let rise until double, about 45 minutes. Bake at 375 degrees for 35 to 45 minutes, until golden. Cool on a wire rack. Makes 2 loaves.

Abigail Smith
Upper Sandusky, OH

Abigail's Crusty White Bread

Southern Hushpuppies

Southern Hushpuppies

This recipe was handed down from my mama... it's the only one she ever used. These are a yummy side served with fried catfish!

1 c. white cornmeal
½ c. all-purpose flour
1½ to 2 T. sugar
1 t. salt
2 T. baking powder
¾ c. buttermilk
1 egg, beaten
1 onion, chopped
Optional: 1 jalapeño pepper,
    seeded and chopped
peanut oil for frying

In a large bowl, combine cornmeal, flour, sugar, salt and baking powder. Add remaining ingredients except oil. Mixture will be thick but should not be dry. If dry, add a little more buttermilk. Heat a deep fryer of peanut oil to 350 degrees. Carefully drop batter from a small spoon. Fry in small batches until dark golden on all sides. Drain on paper towels. Serves 8 to 10.

Cora Phillips
Ozark, AL

Bake up a batch of Abigail's Crusty White Bread to serve on Christmas day. Slice it in thick pieces and serve with plenty of butter! They'll all be asking for more Southern Hushpuppies. Add a little chopped jalapeño to the batter for an extra bit of kick and flavor.

Party Bubble Bread

This is fabulous on Christmas Eve.

$1/2$ c. butter, melted
$1^1/2$ c. shredded Mexican-blend
    cheese
$1/4$ c. shredded mozzarella cheese
10-oz. jar sliced jalapeno
    peppers, drained
1 t. dried parsley
2 12-oz. tubes refrigerated
    biscuits cut into quarters

In a large bowl, combine butter, cheeses, pepper slices and parsley; add biscuits and toss to coat. Transfer to an ungreased Bundt pan. Bake at 350 degrees for 30 minutes, or until golden. Invert onto a serving plate; serve warm. Serves 8.

Amy Hunt
Traphill, NC

Buttermilk Cinnamon Rolls

3 c. all-purpose flour
4 t. baking powder
$1/4$ t. baking soda
1 t. salt
$1/2$ c. shortening
$1^1/2$ c. buttermilk
$1/2$ c. margarine, softened
$1/2$ c. sugar
$1/2$ t. cinnamon
Optional: Powdered Sugar Icing
    (page 94), crushed peppermint
    candies

Combine first 4 ingredients; cut in shortening until crumbs form. Stir in buttermilk until well blended; knead dough on a lightly floured surface for 4 to 5 minutes. Roll out to $1/4$-inch thickness; spread margarine over dough to edges. In a small bowl, mix sugar and cinnamon; sprinkle over dough. Roll up jelly-roll style; cut into $1/2$-inch slices. Place on a greased baking sheet; bake at 450 degrees for 10 to 12 minutes. Makes about one dozen.

Dobie Hill
Lubbock, TX

Party Bubble Bread

Buttermilk
Cinnamon Rolls

Cranberry
Upside-Down
Muffins

Having a holiday party? Serve some cheesy Party Bubble Bread for a quick appetizer. Everyone loves Buttermilk Cinnamon Rolls! Need a pretty breakfast treat? Make some Cranberry Upside-Down Muffins to share!

Cranberry Upside-Down Muffins

Served warm, these tangy muffins are delicious alongside savory soups and stews.

$2^{1}/_{2}$ c. all-purpose flour
$^{1}/_{2}$ c. sugar
1 T. baking powder
$^{1}/_{2}$ t. salt
$1^{1}/_{4}$ c. milk
$^{1}/_{3}$ c. butter, melted
1 egg, beaten

Combine flour, sugar, baking powder and salt in a large bowl; mix well. Add milk, butter and egg; stir just until moistened. Set aside. Prepare Cranberry Topping; spoon into 18 greased muffin cups. Spoon batter over topping, filling each cup $^{2}/_{3}$ full. Bake at 400 degrees for 20 to 25 minutes, until a toothpick tests clean. Immediately invert onto a wire rack set over wax paper; serve warm. Makes $1^{1}/_{2}$ dozen.

Cranberry Topping:
$^{1}/_{4}$ c. brown sugar, packed
$^{1}/_{4}$ c. butter
$^{1}/_{2}$ t. cinnamon
$^{1}/_{2}$ c. cranberries, halved
Optional: $^{1}/_{2}$ c. chopped nuts

Combine ingredients in a small saucepan. Cook over medium heat until brown sugar is dissolved.

Barbara Girlardo
Pittsburgh, PA

Sweet Desserts

What better way to say "Merry Christmas" than to serve a beautiful dessert all dressed up for the holidays! Layering slices of pound cake with ruby red cranberries is the trick to making Holiday Cranberry Trifle. Christmas cookies are everyone's favorite so stir up a batch of Pistachio Wreath Cookies or Old-Fashioned Sugar Cookies. After Christmas caroling, warm up their tummies with Buttermilk Pear Cobbler and some hot tea. Want a show-stopping dessert this year? Create your holiday masterpiece by baking a Peppermint 7-Layer Cake. Stack the pink and white layers and top them with cream cheese frosting and cut-out cookies. You'll love creating these sweet desserts!

Holiday Cranberry Trifle

This dessert is so beautiful. I love to entertain with it...a perfect centerpiece for the holiday season. Delicious with either fresh or frozen cranberries.

2 12-oz. pkgs. fresh cranberries
2$\frac{1}{4}$ c. sugar, divided
zest of 1 orange
2 c. water
8-oz. pkg. cream cheese,
    softened
$\frac{1}{4}$ c. light brown sugar, packed
$\frac{1}{2}$ t. vanilla extract
2 c. whipping cream
2 all-butter pound cakes, cut into
    $\frac{3}{4}$-inch thick slices

In a medium saucepan, combine cranberries, 2 cups sugar, zest and water. Bring to a simmer over medium heat; cook until cranberries begin to burst, about 8 to 10 minutes. Remove from heat; let cool completely. Using an electric mixer on high speed, beat cream cheese, brown sugar, remaining sugar and vanilla until well combined. With electric mixer on medium speed, gradually add cream; continue beating until soft peaks form. Arrange $\frac{1}{3}$ of cake slices in a 3-quart clear glass serving dish. Spoon $\frac{1}{3}$ of cranberry mixture over cake; spread to sides of dish. Dollop $\frac{1}{3}$ of cream cheese mixture over cranberry mixture; spread to sides of dish. Repeat twice, ending with cream cheese mixture, reserving some cranberry mixture for the top of the cake. Cover and refrigerate at least 2 hours before serving. Serves 12.

Sonya Labbe
Los Angeles, CA

Cherries Jubilee Crisp

This recipe makes just a few portions so it's great for small families.

17-oz. can sweet cherries
2 T. orange liqueur or
    orange juice
2$\frac{1}{2}$ t. cornstarch
$\frac{1}{4}$ c. quick-cooking oats,
    uncooked
6 T. all-purpose flour
$\frac{1}{4}$ c. brown sugar, packed
$\frac{1}{4}$ t. nutmeg
$\frac{1}{4}$ c. cold butter, diced
Garnish: whipped cream, nutmeg

Combine undrained cherries, liqueur or juice and cornstarch in a saucepan. Cook and stir over medium heat until cornstarch dissolves and mixture is thickened, about 2 minutes. Pour into a lightly greased one-quart casserole dish; let cool for 10 minutes. In a small bowl, stir together oats, flour, brown sugar and nutmeg. Add butter; mix with a fork until crumbly. Sprinkle oat mixture over cherry mixture. Bake, uncovered, at 375 degrees for about 20 minutes, until topping is golden. Serve warm, topped with whipped cream and a sprinkle of nutmeg. Serves 4.

Jill Valentine
Jackson, TN

Cherries Jubilee Crisp

Pistachio Wreath Cookies

Pistachio Wreath Cookies

My family loves this recipe! We make it every year for a Christmas treat!

2 c. all-purpose flour
$\frac{1}{4}$ t. baking powder
$\frac{1}{4}$ t. salt
$\frac{3}{4}$ c. butter
$\frac{3}{4}$ c. sugar
1 egg, beaten
$\frac{1}{2}$ t. vanilla extract
$\frac{1}{2}$ t. almond extract
$\frac{1}{4}$ c. pistachios, coarsely chopped
$\frac{1}{4}$ t. green food coloring
Garnish: red cinnamon candies,
    icing

In a large bowl, combine flour, baking powder and salt. In a separate bowl, beat butter until softened; add sugar and beat until fluffy. Add egg, extracts and pistachios. Add butter mixture to flour mixture; mix well. Divide dough in half. Add green food coloring to one half; mix well. Keeping dough separate, wrap in plastic wrap and chill for at least 30 minutes. On a lightly floured surface, roll about a tablespoon of plain dough into a 6-inch rope. Repeat with green dough. Place ropes side-by-side and twist together 6 times. Shape twisted dough in a circle; gently pinch ends together. Place on an ungreased baking sheet. Repeat steps until no dough remains. Bake at 375 degrees for 10 minutes. Cool on wire racks. Add red candies using a dot of icing. Makes 12 to 15 cookies.

Natasha Spillett
Alberta, Canada

Buttermilk Pear Cobbler

Cherries Jubilee Crisp has an oatmeal topping that is sweet and crispy. Twist up some Pistachio Wreath Cookies in no time! Buttermilk Pear Cobbler will warm their hearts and their tummies!

Buttermilk Pear Cobbler

This recipe was inspired by my Grandmother Doris. It is a country cobbler topped with a lightly sweetened, soft buttermilk biscuit. Absolute comfort food!

3 lbs. Anjou or Bosc pears, peeled, cored and sliced
1/3 c. brown sugar, packed
1 T. all-purpose flour
1 T. lemon juice
1 t. cinnamon
1/4 t. nutmeg
1/4 t. mace

Combine all ingredients in a large bowl; toss gently to coat pears. Spoon pear mixture into an 8"x8" baking pan coated with non-stick vegetable spray. Drop Biscuit Topping by heaping tablespoonfuls onto pear mixture. Bake at 350 degrees for 45 minutes, or until lightly golden and bubbly. Makes 8 servings.

Biscuit Topping:
1 c. all-purpose flour
1 T. baking powder
3 T. buttermilk
2 T. sugar
1/2 c. chilled butter
3/4 c. milk

In a bowl, mix together flour, baking powder, buttermilk and sugar. Cut in butter with a fork until mixture is crumbly; add milk and mix well.

Trysha Mapley
Palmer, AK

Old-Fashioned Sugar Cookies

Oh how Santa will love Old-Fashioned Sugar Cookies on Christmas Eve! Create a beautiful Upside-Down Apple-Pecan Pie and it will become the centerpiece of your holiday table.

Old-Fashioned Sugar Cookies

This is an old recipe handed down in my twin sister's husband's family for generations. This is the perfect cookie dough for making Christmas cookies for Santa.

1/3 c. butter, softened
1/3 c. shortening
1 c. all-purpose flour
3/4 c. sugar
1 egg, beaten
1 T. milk
1 t. baking powder
1 t. vanilla extract
1/8 t. salt
Powdered Sugar Icing

In a large bowl, beat butter and shortening with an electric mixer on medium speed for 30 seconds. Add remaining ingredients; mix well. Cover and chill dough for 3 hours. On a lightly floured surface, roll out dough to a 1/8-inch thickness; cut into desired shapes with cookie cutters. Arrange on ungreased baking sheets. Bake at 375 degrees for 7 minutes, or until golden. Frost with Powdered Sugar Icing (page 94) and decorate as desired. Makes 2 dozen.

Kris Kellis
Salisbury, NC

Upside-Down Apple-Pecan Pie

When I was a child, both my grandmas used to make this pie. Nana gave Granny the recipe and they took turns making it for holidays. Over the years, I tweaked it and even won the North Carolina State Apple Cook-Off Grand Champion with it. You can use any mix of sweet and tart cooking apples.

½ c. butter, softened
1½ c. pecan halves
1½ c. brown sugar, packed
2 9-inch pie crusts
½ c. sugar
2 T. lemon juice
1 t. vanilla extract
3 T. all-purpose flour
1 T. apple pie spice
1⅛ t. cinnamon
½ t. nutmeg

3 c. Honey Crisp apples, peeled, cored and sliced
3 c. Swiss Gourmet apples, peeled, cored and sliced
Garnish: vanilla ice cream

Spread softened butter in the bottom and up the sides of a 9" deep-dish pie plate. Arrange pecan halves over butter, flat-side up, to cover pie plate. Sprinkle brown sugar over pecans. Place one pie crust on top of brown sugar; press into pie plate and set aside. In a large bowl, combine sugar, lemon juice, vanilla, flour and spices; mix well. Add apples and toss until coated. Spoon apple mixture evenly into pie crust. Cover with remaining pie crust; fold over edges and crimp together. (This will be the bottom of the pie, so don't worry about how it looks.) Pierce crust several times with a fork. Bake at 450 degrees for 10 minutes; reduce heat to 350 degrees and bake for another 45 minutes. Remove from oven; let stand briefly until the bubbling stops. While pie is still hot, invert a serving plate over pie and flip pie over onto plate. Pecans will now be on top. Serve warm, topped with scoops of ice cream if desired. Makes 8 servings.

Francine Bryson
Pickens, SC

Upside-Down Apple-Pecan Pie

Peppermint 7-Layer Cake

Peppermint 7-Layer Cake

This cake is so grand and tastes amazing. If you want a show-stopping holiday dessert, this layer cake is it!

18^{1}/$_{4}$-oz. pkg. white cake mix
3 egg whites, beaten
1^{1}/$_{3}$ c. plus ^{1}/$_{2}$ c. buttermilk
2 T. oil
9-oz. pkg. yellow cake mix
1 egg, beaten
1^{1}/$_{2}$ T. baking cocoa
^{1}/$_{2}$ t. baking soda
2 T. red food coloring
1 t. cider vinegar
pink food coloring
1 c. crushed peppermint candy
Optional: Snowflake cookies

In a large bowl, combine dry white cake mix, egg whites, 1^{1}/$_{3}$ cups buttermilk and oil. With an electric mixer on medium speed, beat until well blended. In a separate large bowl, combine dry yellow cake mix and remaining ingredients. Beat with an electric mixer on medium speed until well blended. Color batter so you will have 2 pans of white cake and 1 pan of red cake. **Note:** the middle layer of the cake is frosting. Pour the colored batter into 3 greased and floured 9" round cake pans. Bake at 350 degrees for 22 to 25 minutes, until a wooden toothpick inserted in center comes out clean. Cool in pans on wire racks for 10 minutes. Remove from pans.

To assemble cake, slice each of the cake layers in half crosswise. Make a double batch of Cream Cheese Frosting. Frost between first three layers. Tint 1 cup of the frosting pink and add 2 t. peppermint extract and ^{1}/$_{2}$ cup crushed peppermint candies. Spread over first three layers. Layer the final three layers. Frost top and sides of cake. Pipe snowflakes on sides of cake. Garnish with remaining crushed candies. Add decorated snowflake cookies around cake if desired. Serve immediately; refrigerate leftovers. Serves 10 to 12.

Arlenna Martinez
Long Beach, CA

Peppermint 7-Layer Cake

You'll need a double batch of frosting to create this amazing Peppermint 7-Layer Cake. The cake is colored red and white and baked in round pans. Then it is sliced and layered with a thick layer of frosting in the middle to make the seven layers. To make it even more spectacular, adorn it with decorated snowflake cookies, made using the Old-Fashioned Sugar Cookie recipe. Cut out the cookies using a snowflake cutter and pipe with white frosting.

Cream Cheese Frosting:
8-oz. pkg. cream cheese, softened
1 c. butter, softened
32-oz. pkg. powdered sugar

In a bowl with an electric mixer on medium speed, beat cream cheese and butter until fluffy. Add extract; lower speed and add powdered sugar a little at a time until well blended.

Arlenna Martinez
Long Beach, CA

Old-Fashioned Sugar Cookies

119

★EASY PARTY FAVORITES★

What fun to gather together for the holidays! Whether it is a drop-in party, a traditional open house affair or just getting together after Christmas caroling, spending time together with family & friends is the best! Entertain this year by wowing them with a beautiful Pine Cone Cheese Ball. Or make it casual with Spicy Party Chicken Wings and Pepper Corn Cups. Warm them up with Festive Fireside Meatballs and Spinach-Parmesan Balls. Want to try something with a new flavor twist? Stir up some Figgy Tapenade to serve with crispy toast rounds. Then gather together to share some Christmas Eggnog and toast the most wonderful season of the year!

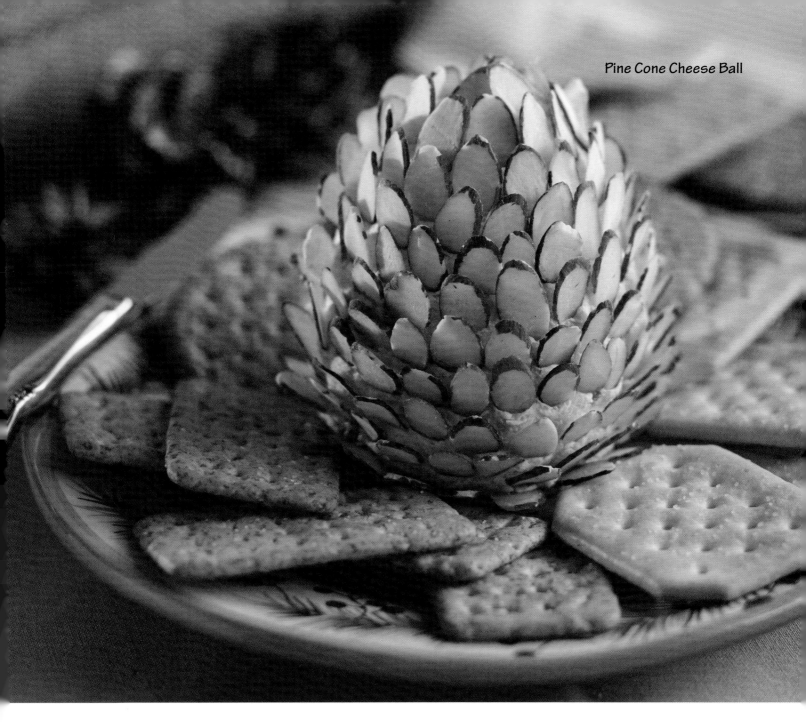

Pine Cone Cheese Ball

Pine Cone Cheese Ball

This cheese ball is easy to assemble and looks so pretty for the holidays! Serve with your favorite crackers.

2 8-oz. pkgs. cream cheese, softened
2 c. shredded sharp Cheddar cheese
1 T. chopped pimentos
1 T onion, chopped
1 T. green pepper, chopped
2 t. Worcestershire sauce
1 t. lemon juice
16-oz. pkg. sliced almonds
assorted crackers

In a bowl, combine cheeses; mix well. Add remaining ingredients except almonds and crackers; mix well. Divide cheese mixture into 2 portions. Wrap each tightly in plastic wrap; chill until firm. Form into 2 egg-like shapes; cover each with almonds, pressing in to resemble pine cones. Serve with crackers. Serves 10 to 12.

Frances Mertz
Wilmington, OH

Pepper Corn Cups

Pepper Corn Cups

I first made this appetizer for a Christmas party. It has turned into an anytime favorite!

8-oz. round Brie cheese
16-oz. pkg. frozen corn, thawed
1 red pepper, diced
1 green pepper, diced
3 2-oz. pkgs. frozen mini phyllo
    shells, thawed

Trim and discard rind from Brie; cut Brie into cubes. Mix together corn and peppers. Place mini phyllo shells on lightly greased baking sheets; evenly divide corn mixture into shells. Place one cube of Brie on each shell. Bake at 350 degrees for 5 to 8 minutes. Makes 3¾ dozen.

Kimberly Ascroft
Merritt Island, FL

Stuffed Mushrooms

I received this recipe from a friend many years ago. They are a cinch to make and a family favorite at holiday parties. Be prepared to share the recipe...they are delicious!

1 lb. sage-flavored ground pork
    sausage
8-oz. pkg. cream cheese,
    softened
25 to 30 small whole button
    mushrooms, stems removed

Brown sausage in a skillet over medium-high heat; drain. Transfer to a bowl and combine with cream cheese, using a fork to blend thoroughly. Place a rounded teaspoonful of sausage mixture inside each mushroom cap. Place on lightly greased baking sheets. Bake at 350 degrees for 20 to 25 minutes, until heated through. Makes about 2½ dozen.

Linda Harris
Colorado Springs, CO

Spicy Party Chicken Wings

These wings have crispy exteriors and lots of flavor!

30 chicken wings
1 c. all-purpose flour
salt and pepper to taste
1 egg, beaten
$\frac{1}{2}$ c. butter
$\frac{1}{2}$ c. oil
3 T. soy sauce
3 T. water
1 c. sugar
$\frac{1}{2}$ c. vinegar
$\frac{1}{2}$ t. salt
1 T. red pepper flakes

Pat wings dry with a paper towel. In a shallow bowl, combine flour with salt and pepper; place egg in a separate bowl. Dip wings in egg, then in flour mixture. In a skillet over medium-high heat, melt butter and add oil; fry wings in butter mixture, turning often, until crisp. Drain and pat off excess oil. Transfer wings to an ungreased 13"x 9" baking pan. In a bowl, combine remaining ingredients. Drizzle mixture over wings. Bake, uncovered, at 350 degrees for about 45 minutes, tossing wings several times, until liquid evaporates and wings are crisp and cooked through. Serve hot. Serves 6 to 8.

Goreta Brown
Alberta, Canada

So pretty with red and green accents, Pepper Corn Cups will disappear from that holiday tray. They'll all be asking for the recipe for your Spicy Party Chicken Wings. Serve them with your favorite holiday ale.

Spicy Party Chicken Wings

Figgy Tapenade

This is an easy appetizer using figs. Serve with slices of French bread or crackers.

1 c. dried figs, chopped
$\frac{1}{2}$ c. water
1 T. olive oil
2 T. balsamic vinegar
1 t. dried rosemary
1 t. dried thyme
$\frac{1}{4}$ t. cayenne pepper
$\frac{2}{3}$ c. Kalamata olives, chopped
2 cloves garlic, minced
salt and pepper to taste
8-oz. pkg. cream cheese
Optional: $\frac{1}{3}$ c. toasted walnuts, chopped

Combine figs and water in a saucepan over medium heat. Bring to a boil; cook until figs are tender and liquid has cooked down. Remove from heat; stir in olive oil, vinegar, herbs and cayenne pepper. Add olives and garlic; mix well. Season with salt and pepper. Cover; refrigerate for 4 hours to overnight. To serve, unwrap cream cheese; place on a serving plate. Spoon tapenade over top; sprinkle with walnuts if desired. Serves 6.

Jo Ann

Figgy Tapenade

Christmas Eggnog

No one will believe that this eggnog is eggless!

3-oz. pkg. instant French vanilla pudding
4 c. milk, divided
4 c. whipping cream
$\frac{1}{2}$ c. sugar
2 to 4 t. vanilla extract
Garnish: whipping cream, nutmeg

In a large bowl, stir together dry pudding mix and one cup of milk. When mixture begins to thicken, add remaining ingredients except garnish; mix well. Cover and chill. Garnish individual servings with whipped topping and a sprinkle of nutmeg. Makes $\frac{1}{2}$ gallon.

Abi Buening
Grand Forks, ND

Christmas Eggnog

Spinach-Parmesan Balls

Figgy Tapenade has a lovely combination of flavors and brings back the memory of figgy pudding in so many holiday songs! So easy and quick to make, Spinach-Parmesan Balls have just the right amount of heat for the perfect appetizer. Christmas Eggnog is so yummy. . .no one will know that it is made without eggs!

Spinach-Parmesan Balls
I made this appetizer for a Christmas gathering and it was a huge hit.

16-oz. pkg. frozen chopped
    spinach, thawed and drained
5 eggs, beaten
1 onion, minced
2 cloves garlic, minced
$^3/_4$ c. margarine, melted
1 c. shredded Parmesan cheese
$^1/_2$ t. dried thyme
$^1/_2$ t. cayenne pepper
$1^3/_4$ c. Italian-style dry bread
    crumbs
Optional: shredded Parmesan
    cheese

Place spinach in a large bowl. Add remaining ingredients; mix well by hand. Shape into one-inch balls. Place closely together on lightly greased baking sheets. Bake at 350 degrees for 25 minutes. Sprinkle with cheese if desired. Makes $2^1/_2$ to $3^1/_2$ dozen.

Leah Dodson
Covington, KY

Mississippi Fun Dip
When this appetizer was served at my friend's 50th birthday party, it was voted the best by all the guests...even the kids! A long, thick loaf of bread works best.

1 loaf Italian bread
2 8-oz. pkgs. cream cheese,
    softened
1 c. sour cream
2 c. shredded Cheddar cheese
2 c. cooked ham, diced
4-oz. can diced green chiles,
    drained
$^1/_4$ c. green onions, diced
scoop-type corn chips

Slice off top of loaf lengthwise and scoop out the bread inside, reserving bread for dipping. Combine remaining ingredients except corn chips. Blend well and spoon mixture into loaf. Replace top of loaf; wrap in aluminum foil. Bake at 400 degrees for one hour and 15 minutes. Unwrap carefully and remove top of loaf. Serve with corn chips and reserved bread pieces. Serves 8 to 10.

Pat Cornett
Smithfield, VA

Onion soup mix is the secret ingredient in Festive Fireside Meatballs. As yummy as they are pretty, Shrimp Puffs have an English muffin base.

Festive Fireside Meatballs

This recipe was shared with me many years ago at a potluck with the girls from work. I've tasted lots of meatballs over the years, but these top them all!

2 lbs. lean ground beef
1-oz. pkg. onion soup mix
1 egg, beaten
1/4 c. dry bread crumbs
2 c. brown sugar, packed
10-oz. bottle chili sauce
1 1/4 c. regular or non-alcoholic
    beer
salt and pepper to taste
1/2 t. garlic powder
2 t. Worcestershire sauce
3 1/2 T. cornstarch
1/4 c. cold water

In a large bowl, combine beef, soup mix, egg and bread crumbs; mix well. Roll into walnut-sized balls. In a skillet over medium heat, brown meatballs on all sides. Drain on paper towels. In a large saucepan over medium heat, combine remaining ingredients except cornstarch and water. Bring to a boil. Stir cornstarch into cold water; gradually add to mixture in saucepan and cook until thickened. Place meatballs in saucepan; stir to coat. Simmer over low heat for about one hour, or until glazed. Serves 8 to 10.

Janis Parr
Ontario, Canada

Festive Fireside Meatballs

Shrimp Puffs

Shrimp Puffs

My mom has been making this oh-so-simple appetizer since I was a kid. It has that kind of easy '70s feel about it, and I have never tried to update it in any way!

1 c. shredded Cheddar cheese
1 c. mayonnaise
6-oz. can small shrimp, drained
$^1/_8$ to $^1/_4$ t. onion salt
12-oz. pkg. English muffins, split
   in half and cut into quarters
Optional: red pepper, parsley

Mix together cheese, mayonnaise, shrimp and onion salt in a large bowl. Spread cheese mixture evenly across quartered English muffins. Place on aluminum-foil lined baking sheets. Bake at 350 degrees for 10 to 20 minutes, until cheese is melted and puffs are golden. Top with a piece of red pepper and parsley if desired. Makes 4 to 5 dozen.

Tiffani Schulte
Wyandotte, MI

Chicky Popovers

These elegant appetizers are surprisingly simple to make and oh-so-yummy!

8-oz. pkg. cream cheese,
   softened
3 boneless, skinless chicken
   breasts, cooked and shredded
1$^1/_2$ t. sesame seed
$^1/_4$ t. dried parsley
1 T. onion, minced
1 t. garlic, minced
$^1/_2$ c. spinach, finely chopped
Optional: $^1/_2$ c. mushrooms, finely
   chopped
salt and pepper to taste
2 8-oz. tubes refrigerated
   crescent rolls

In a medium bowl, combine all ingredients except crescent rolls; mix well. Open crescent rolls but do not separate into triangles. Instead pair triangles to form 8 squares. Pinch seams together. Spoon chicken mixture evenly over the squares. Fold up corners into center, layering like flower petals so each roll is sealed. Place popovers on a lightly greased baking sheet. Bake at 350 degrees for 12 to 15 minutes, until golden and heated through. Makes 8 servings.

Deanna Lyons
Roswell, GA

127

Project Instructions

Pom-pom Garland

continued from page 10

4. Slide yarn off ruler. Leave the long tie yarn. Cut loops to form pom-pom. Trim edges of yarn as needed to shape pom-pom. Repeat for desired number of pom-poms.

5. Lay purchased ball fringe cut to desired garland length on flat surface. Tie yarn pom-poms onto the ball fringe at desired intervals. (We tied the pom-poms at every third ball on the fringe.)

6. Trim ends of long tie yarn. Fluff pom-poms as needed when hanging.

Friendly Retro Reindeer

continued from page 11

3. Embroider the deer's eye and mouth. Use 3 strands of embroidery floss and embroidery needle to make 2 connected stitches to form an eye at the back of the tan eyepiece. Frame the eye with 2 very small V-shaped eyelashes. Make a single stitch mouth halfway down the deer's chin.

4. Sandwich the cardboard between the sewn front and plain back piece. Use 3 strands of tan floss and begin whip stitching around the outside edge of the deer, trapping both felt layers in each stitch. When you reach the nose, stop to add the pom-pom to the seam.

5. Wrap the felt ribbon around the neck. Cross the ends and lay the bow piece on top. Use 3 strands of red floss and make a large stitch around either side of the bow to attach it to the felt ribbon below.

6. Thread the cording through the top of the felt ribbon on the back. Bring the ends together and tie them in an overhand knot.

Music-Inspired Paper Chain

shown on page 12

- vintage sheet music, music-print scrapbook paper or copyright-free sheet music
- copy machine (optional)
- vellum in white or off-white (optional)
- crafts glue
- scissors

1. Choose the desired paper to make the snowflakes. The paper should not be too heavy, or it will be hard to cut. You can use actual sheets of vintage music. If copying the music to vellum, be sure the music is copyright-free.

2. Cut each paper chain link piece along the bar line of the music, about $1^3/4$" x 6" long.

3. Curl the paper around and secure with glue, making a link. Thread the next paper through the link and glue forming a chain. Continue until desired length of chain is made.

Lacy Snowflakes
continued from page 12

2. Cut the desired paper to measure 4¼" x 11". Accordion fold the piece of paper making each fold about ¾" w. See Photo A.

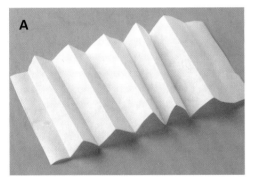

A

3. Fold the pleated paper in half. See Photo B.

B

4. Cut a notch on each side of the middle fold and tie the ribbon around the middle making a knot to secure. See Photo C.

C

5. Use scissors to cut shapes on the folds. If desired, mark shapes first using a pattern. See Photo D. (See page 150 for patterns.)

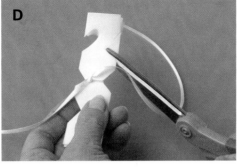

D

6. Put glue on both inside flat pieces. See Photo E.

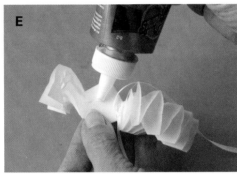

E

7. Pull the glued ends together and hold to secure. See Photo F.

F

8. If desired, mix equal parts of glue and water and brush on the edges of the snowflake. Dust with glitter.

Gingham & Felt Mini Trees
continued from page 13

1. Enlarge and trace the patterns (page 152) and cut out. Cut 3 fabric and felt pieces for each tree. Lay a fabric triangle over a felt triangle. Group 3 same-sized pairs together for each tree.

2. Working on the right side of the fabric, machine stitch 2 sides together. Machine stitch down one side of the pairs, top to bottom. Open the connected pair and stack the third pair under one of the unattached sides; machine stitch the side together. Open the tree, line up and sew the 2 remaining open sides. Trim away excess fabric with pinking shears.

3. Reach inside the connected tree to stitch buttons to all 3 sides, arranging buttons as desired.

4. Use a pencil end or knitting needle to push stuffing up into the very top, then fill the rest of the tree.

5. Cut the 3 different sized base template patterns out of white felt. Pin one to each corresponding stuffed tree. Place both the end of the sides and the base under the presser foot and machine stitch all around the outside edge. Trim away the excess fabric with pinking shears.

6. Cut 2 small circles from felt. Sandwich the circles between 2 buttons. Hand stitch the buttons together catching the felt in the stitches. Hot-glue to top of tree.

129

Christmas Carol Table Runner
continued from page 14

Prepare the Appliqué Pieces
1. Copy and trace patterns (page 148). Trace the holly leaves on the paper side of paper-backed fusible web, tracing the number of times indicated on the pattern, making the reverse of some leaves as indicated. (Patterns are the reverse of the finished design.) Mark the leaf pattern numbers near one edge.
2. Cut around the pattern pieces about $1/4$" outside the traced lines. If desired, remove the fusible web from the center of the pattern pieces by cutting about $1/4$" inside the traced line. This will give the finished appliqué a softer feel.
3. Referring to the paper-backed fusible web directions and the Placement Illustration (page 149) fuse 7 or 8 leaf patterns to the wrong side of each shade of green fabric. Cut out on the traced lines.

Prepare the Holly Berries
1. Cut 10 Berry circles from the red check.
2. Cut a 1" strip off the short edge of the batting rectangle. Cut 10 Berry Padding circles from this strip.
3. Using a strong thread take small running stitches about $1/4$" from the edge of a red check circle. Pull the

thread to slightly gather circle with right side of fabric facing out.
4. Slip a circle of batting into the center of the circle. Pull the thread to gather over the batting making a circle the size of the batting. Take a few backstitches to hold the gathers. Make 10 berries.

Quilting the Background
1. Trace the Quilting Curve pattern (Page 148) 3 times on tracing or tissue paper. Cut out about $1/2$" from both sides of the lines and tape together matching the short lines to form a long wave. See Illustration 1.

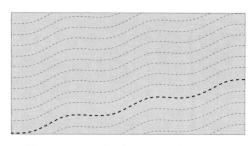

Illustration 1: First Marked Line

2. Use this line to mark the quilting lines on the background. Start the first line at the lower left corner and end about $7 1/2$" above lower right corner. Mark the remaining lines $1 1/2$" away from the previous line in both directions.
3. Layer the marked background, batting and backing. Quilt on the marked lines. Then parallel quilt about $1/8$" above five lines starting with the first line above the left corner. See Illustration 2.

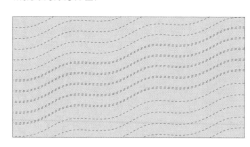

Illustration 2: Quilting Lines

Arrange the Appliqué
1. Referring to the Placement Illustration (page 149) remove paper backing from the holly leaves, arrange and fuse on a non-stick pressing sheet making 3 clusters. Remove paper backing, arrange and fuse each note on a non-stick pressing sheet. Arrange the holly leaves and notes on the background. Fuse in place.

Stitch the Appliqué
1. Using a matching color of thread, stitch around each leaf and note with a small zigzag stitch or a narrow satin zigzag stitch.
2. Stitch veins in the holly leaves.
3. Hand appliqué 3 or 4 berries in the center of each leaf cluster.

Finish the Quilt
1. Trim the top to 16" x 32" straightening the edges and squaring the corners.
2. Join together the binding strips with diagonal seams to make a continuous strip. Use to bind the quilt.

Evergreen Welcome
shown on page 15
Little evergreen trees are tucked into silver pails for a real country welcome.

- silver pails
- small evergreen trees
- dirt if required
- purchased berry pokes
- red-and-white checked ribbon

1. Center the trees in the pails, adding more dirt to secure if needed.
2. Poke berries into the greenery. Tie the ribbon around the pails.

Cheery Cherry Tote Bag
shown on page 19
Brightly patterned oil cloth makes a generous tote bag for carrying holiday goodies.

- 1 yard black print oil cloth
- $1/2$ yard white print oil cloth
- $1/2$ yard teal print oil cloth
- scissors
- matching sewing thread
- sewing machine
- clips

1. Cut the following pieces from the oil cloth prints:

Black Oil Cloth
2 pieces 20" x 20" (Body)
1 piece 5" x 20" (Bag Bottom)

White Oil Cloth
2 pieces 15" x 20" (Large pockets)

Aqua Oil Cloth
2 pieces 8 ½" x 7" (Small Pockets)
2 pieces 8 ½" x 14" (Side Pieces)
2 pieces 6" x 36" (Straps)

2. Hem top of aqua pockets with 1" hem. Angle cut corners. Hem top of white pockets with 2" hem. Turn under $1/2$" on remaining 3 sides of aqua pockets. Pin to white pocket, centering top to bottom and side to side. Stitch in place.
3. Pin white/aqua pockets to black body pieces at sides and bottom.

4. Stitch aqua side pieces to black bottom piece at short seams. Pin gusset to body of bag with right sides together. Stitch, pivoting at lower corners. Turn, DO NOT press.
5. Make straps by folding 36" long piece in half with ½" turned under at both edges. Topstitch all long edges.
6. Fold down top edge of bag 3". Use clips to hold. Pin straps to bag evenly at top edge, having raw edge of strap even with raw edge of turn back. Topstitch catching straps. Reinforce stitch at top edge of bag over straps.

Yummy First Foods Bib
continued from page 20
5. Embroider the words and around the fused pieces following the pattern and chart (page 147) using desired embroidery stitches.
6. Prepare the binding by cutting a 1" piece of stripe fabric on the bias. Set aside.
7. Lay the back and finished front with wrong sides together. Sandwich the lightweight batting between the pieces having all edges even. Bind the edges of the bib.
8. Sew the adhesive fastener tape to the back of the bib for closers.

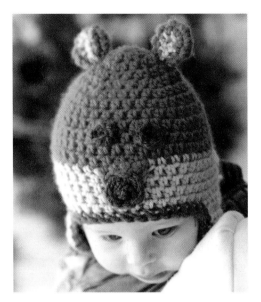

Foxy Baby Hat

continued from page 21

For Hat Body using orange yarn:
ROW 1: Ch 2. Crochet 6sc in 2nd ch from hook. Join with a sl st to first ch st.
ROW 2: Ch 2, hdc in same st, 2hdc in next st and each around. Join with sl st to top of beg.
ROW 3: Ch2, 2 hdc in next st, hdc in next, repeating pattern around hat. Join with sl st to top of beg.
ROW 4: Ch 2, 2hdc in next st, around hat. Join with sl st top of beg.
ROWS 5-11: Ch 2, hdc in each st around hat.
Continue to desired height, then join with sl st and fasten off.

For Lower Hat Body using light grey yarn:
ROWS 12-15: Sl st where orange yarn ended to join. Ch 2, hdc around hat, then join with sl st after row 15 and fasten off.

For Ear Flaps, using light grey yarn:
ROW 1: On side of hat, where you would like flap to begin, join with sl st. Continue to join to hat, stitching 8 hdc.
ROWS 2-4: Ch 2 at the beg of each row. Dec at the beg and end of each row, using hdc, until only 2 sts remain. Repeat on opposite side of hat.

For Hat Trim using dark grey yarn:
ROW 1: Sl st to join to hat, hdc around hat, then join with sl st.
ROW 2: Sc around hat, then join with sl st and fasten off.

For Nose Tips & Eyes using dark grey yarn:
Ch 4. Join with sl st to first ch st to form ring. Sc 8 st into center of ring. Ch 2, 2 hdc in each st.
When desired diameter of circle is reached, join with sl st and fasten off. Create 3 circles, 2 for eyes and one for the nose.

For Nose using orange yarn:
ROW 1: Ch 6.
ROWS 2-3: Ch 2 at the beg of each row. Dec at the beg and end of each row, using hdc, until only 2 sts remain.

For Ears using light grey and orange yarn:
Ch 4. Join with sl st to first ch st to form ring.
Sc 8 st into center of ring. Ch 2, 2hdc in each st around circle, join with sl st and fasten off.

Join orange yarn with sl st where light grey yarn ended. Ch 2, 2hdc in each st around circle twice. Join with sl st and fasten off. Repeat to create 2 ears.

Assembly and finishing:
When all pieces are made, join ears, eyes and nose pieces to hat using a needle and same color of yarn.

Grandmother's Beaded Bracelet

continued from page 22

4. Using the crimping tool, squeeze the crimp bead until flat to keep the wire from slipping out.
5. String the beads in the order of the design you have planned. Thread over both wires up to the crimp bead and continue stringing until you reach the desired length, ending the design with another crimp bead. Leave at least 4" of wire remaining to attach the other end of the clasp.
6. Loop the end of the wire back through the other end of the clasp and back through the crimp bead. Squeeze with crimping tool to secure. Feed the wire tail through at least 2 of the beads and cut off the excess wire with wire cutters.

Buttons & Bows Wraps

shown on page 22
Bakers' twine, buttons and bows combine to make easy holiday wraps.

- wrapped or colored boxes
- bakers' twine
- vintage or new buttons

- ¼" w ribbon
- crafts glue
- purchased gift tags

1. Wrap the bakers' twine around the box as desired, crisscrossing or double wrapping the twine. Thread the buttons through the twine while wrapping if desired.

2. Make tiny bows using the ribbon. Glue buttons and bows where the bakers' twine crosses. Tie on a gift tag if desired.

Felt Package Toppers
shown on page 23
Little pieces of felt are layered to create holly and poinsettia shapes.

- wrapped package
- tracing paper
- pencil
- scissors
- red and green felt
- jingle bells
- patterned ribbon
- hot-glue gun and hot glue
- transparent tape
- fine-line red permanent marker

1. Copy the leaf patterns (page 155) onto tracing paper. Cut out.

2. Trace around the shapes onto the green and red felt. Cut out. Use the red marker to make fine lines on the poinsettia leaves.

3. Wrap the ribbon around the package and secure in the back with tape.

4. Layer the red leaves to resemble a poinsettia and hot-glue in place. Glue jingle bells to the center.

5. Hot-glue the holly leaves along the edge of the ribbon. Glue jingle bells in groups of 3 at the top of the leaves.

Sticks & Stones Swag
shown from page 26
Combine sticks and stones and a variety of greenery for a stunning Christmas swag.

- fresh evergreen swag
- flat stones
- 24 gauge copper wire
- wire cutters
- sticks
- pinecones
- berry pokes

1. Wrap the stones with wire leaving tails for attaching. Set aside.

2. Tie a bow with the ribbon using wire, leaving a tail for attaching. Set aside.

3. Lay the swag on a flat surface. Arrange the sticks on top and wire in place. Arrange the stones and pinecones and wire in place. Add the bow and a wire for hanging.

Buche De Noel
continued from page 27
1. Trim the log to 14" long, trimming off one rounded side so it lays flat. **Note:** Our log was 3" in diameter. Drill four ⅞" holes along the top rounded side leaving 1½" between the holes.

2. To make the mushroom caps, work over wax paper. Condition the polymer clay with your hands until it is soft and pliable. Roll walnut-sized balls and then flatten them slightly against the work surface. Be sure the tops retain their rounded shape. Add a few larger and smaller sized caps for variety. **TIP:** Carefully wash the red dye out of your fingertips before continuing to the next step.

(continued on page 134)

(continued from page 133)

3. Working over a fresh piece of wax paper, pinch very tiny sections of clay and roll them into tiny balls. They should be sunflower-seed size and smaller. Once you've rolled a generous assortment of spots, push them directly onto the tops of the caps. They should spread to $1/8$" to $1/2$" w. Mix different sized spots and arrange them randomly over the caps.

4. Roll $1/2$" to 1" white coils for the mushroom stems. Use the wider coil sections for the bigger caps and the smaller ones for the smaller caps.

TIP: Carefully hold the prepared caps in one hand while you attach the top of the coil to the underside with the other hand. This will keep the red dye in one hand and prevent it from transferring to the white stems.

Use a spoon end to blend the clay at the top of the coil into the cap if desired. Press the finished mushroom gently down onto the work surface. This will flatten the clay at the bottom of the stem and assure the mushroom will stand upright.

5. Transfer all the mushrooms so that they are standing upright in a baking dish. Follow the package directions to cure the clay in the oven. Let the baked mushrooms cool before handling.

6. Insert candles into the prepared log, and surround the log with fresh evergreen pieces and clay mushrooms.

Never leave a burning candle unattended.

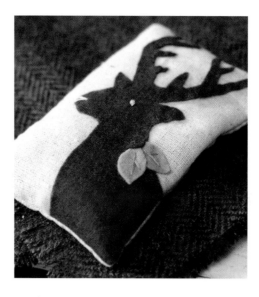

Woodland Sachets

continued from page 28

3. Pin, then hand stitch a felt silhouette to each muslin front. Make small stitches with sewing thread; your stitches should sink into the felt and hide in the fibers. Work your way around the outside edge making sure that the entire animal, antlers, ears and feet are all securely attached.

4. Decorate the animals with the berries and leaves. Embroider the berries in place with a single red floss Cross Stitch, then attach the leaf with a single green floss Straight Stitch. (See page 143 for Embroidery Stitches.)

5. Placing right sides together, stack the decorated front over the gingham back. Machine stitch around the outside edge of sachet, leaving $1 1/2$" opening. Trim the corners and turn the sachet right side out.

6. Roll a sheet of paper into a funnel. Insert the narrow end into the sachet opening and use the funnel to insert 1 to $1 1/2$ cups of balsam lavender mixture into the sachet. Tuck the fabric edges into the sachet and stitch the opening closed. Use sewing needle and off-white thread to sew the opening closed.

Evergreen Print Greeting Cards

shown on page 29
Let nature give you the patterns to print lovely holiday greeting cards.

- blank greeting cards and envelopes in desired colors
- fresh evergreen
- disposable plate
- message rubber stamp
- ink pad
- pencil with new eraser
- acrylic paint in desired colors
- waxed paper
- plain paper (optional)
- fine glitter (optional)

1. Lay the card and envelope on the waxed paper and plan the design, practicing first on a plain piece of paper if desired.

2. Stamp the message using the rubber stamp and ink pad. Let dry.

3. Place desired color of paint on the disposable plate. Flatten and dip the evergreen into the paint. Stamp the design on the card front where desired. If using glitter, dust immediately. Let dry.

4. To make little berries, dip the end of a new pencil eraser into the paint and stamp onto the paper. Let dry.

Cable Sweater Stocking

continued from page 32

4. For hanging loop, turn in long edges of loop, bringing long edges to center. Fold in half and stitch close to long open edge. Fold loop in half and baste to upper back edge of stocking on lining side. Whip stitch lining in place at top of stocking.

5. For cuff, use desired area of sweater fabric to cut a 5"x17" piece of fabric for cuff. Finish short edges of cuff if needed.

6. Place the right side of the cuff on the wrong side of stocking, centering the middle of cuff at the center back of the stocking. With the raw edges even, sew the cuff to the stocking. Fold the cuff to the right side of the stocking. Press.

7. Make a large covered button using the button kit and plaid flannel scrap. Sew to the side of the cuff.

Pom-Pom Cuff Stocking and Red-Plaid Flannel Stocking

shown on page 32
Soft, plaid flannel stitches up into welcoming stockings for Santa to fill.

- photocopier or scanner
- pencil
- scissors
- 1/2 yard of flannel in desired color and pattern
- 1/2 yard contrast fabric with light body or stiffness (for lining)
- 22" of cream pom-pom trim (for Pom-Pom Cuff Stocking)
- white tassel and 2 buttons (for Red-Plaid Flannel Stocking)
- 2 1/3" x7" strip of fabric for loop
- sewing machine
- matching sewing thread

What you do for both stockings:

1. Enlarge stocking pattern (page 156) and cut out. Cut out pattern pieces from appropriate fabrics. In addition, cut a 10"x15" piece of fabric for cuff.

2. Stitch stocking pieces with right sides together, leaving top edge open, using 1/4" seam. Clip curves. Turn right side out.

3. Stitch lining pieces with right sides together, using 3/8" seam.

Trim the seam close to stitching to reduce bulk in stocking.

4. Turn in long edges of loop, bringing long edges to center. Fold in half and stitch close to long open edge. Insert lining inside turned stocking, keeping top straight edges even. Fold loop in half and baste to upper back edge of stocking on lining side.

5. Stitch ends of cuff, right sides together. Turn. Fold in half with raw edges even. Pin right side of cuff to wrong side of stocking. Stitch. Turn cuff to outside, folding only half way down. Press stocking body lightly.

6. For Pom-Pom Cuff Stocking, hand stitch pom-poms to middle of cuff. **For Red-Plaid Flannel Stocking,** sew buttons and tassel to cuff at side.

Flannel Trees

continued from page 36

1. Trace patterns (page 146) and cut out. You'll need 2 flannel pieces and 2 fleece linings for each tree. Cut the lining pieces 1/4" smaller on all sides than the main pieces. Follow manufacturer's instructions to adhere the fleece to the center of each flannel tree piece.

2. Pin the lined tree pieces right sides together. Machine stitch around the tree starting and ending on either side of the base. Leave the

(continued on page 136)

(continued from page 135)

base open. Turn the tree right side out. Use needle and thread to stitch bells over the front of the tree or to each limb end.

3. Stuff the tree slightly and insert the branch into the opening, breaking off the branch to desired length. Remove branch. Hand stitch the opening closed stopping halfway to insert the branch end. Squeeze in a little glue to anchor the branch in place. Continue sewing the rest of the tree base closed.

4. Create the hanging loop using the leather cording, sewing it to the tree top. Make a tiny bow from the suede lace. Hot-glue the bow at the top, covering the connection.

Easy Sticker Cards
shown on page 40
So simple to make, you can create dozens in an evening!

- purchased blank cards
- stickers in desired designs
- alphabet stickers
- scissors

1. Plan the design of the cards before beginning. Plan the message of the card and adhere in place.
2. Surround with desired stickers, cutting off the border sticker ends with scissors.

Burlap & Berry Wreath
shown on page 45
Welcome them with this country wreath.

- purchased fresh 28" evergreen wreath
- 5 yards of 2^1/$_2$" red-trimmed burlap ribbon
- 4 yards of 2" red-and-cream-checked ribbon
- purchased berry pokes
- pinecones
- ^{1}/$_2$ yard red burlap
- Six 2" foam balls such as Styrofoam
- rubber bands
- 24 gauge wire
- wire cutters
- scissors
- 3 large red jingle bells
- red and natural twine

1. For the burlap ball, cut a 8"x 8" piece of burlap and wrap around foam ball. Pull burlap around ball and secure with rubber band. Wrap red twine around rubber band. Fringe the end of the burlap. Make 6 balls. Set aside.
2. Wrap the wreath with the checked ribbon and secure with wire.
3. Wire berry pokes and pinecones into wreath. Thread jingle bells onto twine and tie at top of wreath. Tuck burlap balls into the greenery and wire if necessary.
4. Tie a bow using the burlap ribbon and wire into the top of the wreath.

Burlap Flower Trims
continued from page 48

1. Trace the pattern (page 146) and cut out. Cut 2 pieces for each flower. In addition, cut a 26"x1^1/$_2$" piece of burlap for the flower center.
2. Layer the shaped pieces and tack in the middle using matching thread.
3. Fold long burlap piece in half, tucking ends in. Using a running stitch, sew stitches near raw edges. Pull the thread up to gather, coiling the piece around to form the flower middle. Tack with thread to secure.
4. Tack the coiled center to the layered pieces. Hand stitch to secure. Sew a button to the center of the flower. Add a twine loop for a hanger if desired.

Country Welcome Pillow
continued from page 49
1. Cut the following pieces:
Two 12"x18" pieces of ticking stripe fabric with stripes running horizontally on pillow.

7" x 12" piece from the vintage towel

12" x 2$\frac{1}{2}$" piece of burlap

12" piece of crocheted trim

2. Stamp muslin scrap with the Christmas stamp. Cut the fabric into a 3" x 5" piece.

3. Fray one edge of burlap pulling threads loose on one long edge using a T-pin. Set aside. Fray edges of stamped piece in same manner.

4. Press $\frac{1}{2}$" seam on one long edge of towel fabric. Position stamped muslin on towel section at top center. Top stitch in place.

5. Layer burlap and crocheted trim with long edges even. Baste. Baste folded edge of towel to trims. Place on top of ticking stripe, making sure edges are even. Topstitch folded edge through all layers to secure trimmed piece to ticking. Baste other 3 edges.

6. Place back of pillow and pillow front right sides together. Stitch around perimeter leaving a space for turning. Turn, press and stuff pillow. Whip stitch opening closed.

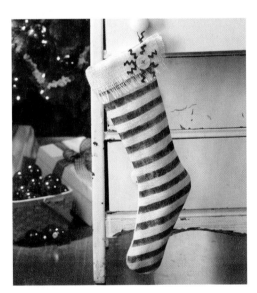

Striped Burlap Stocking

continued from page 50

5. Stitch stocking pieces with right sides together, leaving top edge open, using $\frac{1}{4}$" seam. Clip curves. Turn right side out.

6. Stitch lining pieces with right sides together, using $\frac{3}{8}$" seam. Trim the seam close to stitching to reduce bulk in stocking. Insert lining inside turned stocking, keeping top straight edges even. Pin right side of cuff to inside lining of stocking and stitch, leaving cuff ends open. Turn cuff to outside of stocking and press. Fringe long and short edges of cuff.

7. Make a rickrack hanging loop and tack to inside of stocking. Crisscross rickrack scraps on cuff and sew button on top.

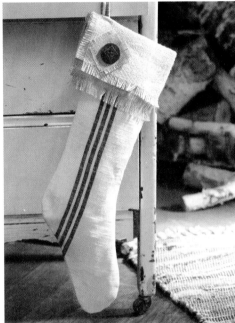

Kitchen Towel Stocking

continued from page 51

2. Stitch the stocking pieces with right sides together, leaving top edge open, using $\frac{1}{4}$" seam. Clip curves. Turn right side out.

3. Stitch lining pieces with right sides together, using $\frac{3}{8}$" seam. Trim the seam close to stitching to reduce bulk in stocking. Insert lining inside turned stocking, keeping top straight edges even. Layer the 2 cuff pieces, and pin the right side of cuffs to inside lining of stocking. Stitch, leaving cuff ends open. Turn cuff to

outside of stocking and press. Fringe long and short edges of cuff.

4. Make a loop and tack to inside of stocking. Cut a small square of gray burlap, fringe edge and tack to the cuff. Sew a button to the burlap.

Fun Cupcake Liner Wreath

shown on page 57

So frilly and pretty, this paper wreath is filled with fun!

- 12" foam wreath such as Styrofoam
- paper cupcake liners in a variety of green colors and prints
- pencil
- red jingle bells
- hot-glue gun and glue sticks
- 1$\frac{1}{2}$" w ribbon for hanging

1. Separate the cupcake liners. Use a pencil to make a small hole in the wreath form. Wrap the liner around the pencil and push into the hole. Add a dot of hot glue if needed.

2. Continue until all of the wreath is covered, putting the liners as close together as possible. Glue the jingle bells into some of the liners. Add a ribbon for hanging.

Happy Clothespin Elves
continued from page 61

1. Trace and cut the patterns (page 150) out of coordinating felt colors. Each elf will need a hat, pant, coat, collar, shoe piece and 2 ears.
2. Paint the eyes onto the clothespin head using black paint.
3. Wrap the pants around the lower half of the pin, overlapping them in the back. Insert a little glue under the overlapped flap to hold in place. Wrap the coat around the top half of the pin, overlapping in the front. Insert glue under the flap to hold in place.
4. Overlap the belt in front, adding a drop of glue to secure. Finish the belt by gluing a sequin buckle on top.
5. Wrap the center of the chenille stem around the neck of the pin. Let the arms extend out either side of the body. Thread a bead hand onto each chenille stem end. Use a dab of glue to hold them in place.
6. Position the collar around the neck over the arm connection, overlapping the last 2 points on the backside; glue them together.
7. Squeeze glue onto the wooden pin base. Stand the glued portion to the back end of the felt shoes.
8. Squeeze glue to the top of the head. Push the pom-pom down over the head. Wrap the hat into a cone shape and test fit over the pom-pom hair. Glue the overlapped cone sides together; glue to the pom-pom. Glue a tiny pom-pom to the hat tip.

138

Sweet Candy Garland
shown on page 61
What could be more fun than strings and strings of sugar candy?

- soft candies or candies with holes
- darning needle
- waxed dental floss
- dish of water

1. Plan the design of the garland by laying the candies on a flat surface.
2. Dip the needle into the water and string the candies onto the floss. Dip and wipe the needle frequently if it becomes sticky. String the candies until the desired length is acheived.

Swirl Cookie Pop Bag
shown on page 65

- brown paper bag with cellophane front (found in the bulk food section of grocery stores)
- scrapbook paper in desired print
- glue stick

- small paper cup
- children's non-toxic clay such as Play Doh
- scissors
- purchased lollipop shape stickers
- cream-color paper
- foam adhesive dots
- decorative scissors
- paper punch
- scrap of red narrow ribbon

1. For the bag, cut strips of patterned cardstock and adhere to the bag front using the glue stick. Add the stickers to the front of the bag using adhesive foam dots. Place some clay into the paper cup and place a cookie pop into the clay to secure. Place cup and cookie pop into the bag. Close the bag.
2. For the tag, copy the printed tag (page 151) on cream-color paper and cut out. Cut a 3"x3" piece of printed cardstock using decorative scissors. Adhere the circle tag to the cardstock front using the glue stick. Add the sticker to the middle of the circle using an adhesive foam dot. Punch a hole in the corner of the cardstock. Thread the ribbon through the hole and attach to the top of the bag.

Pretty Cookie Bar Box
shown on page 67

- purchased box with cellophane window (available in the bakery department at grocery stores)
- waxed paper
- sticker strip
- purchased blank tag

- scrap of paper tape such as Washi tape
- glue stick
- 14" strip of $\frac{1}{4}$" w ribbon

1. Place bars in the box using waxed paper to separate layers. Use the sticker strip to close and seal the box, running the stickers across the top of the box.
2. For the tag, copy the printed tag (page 150) onto white paper and cut out. Adhere to the purchased tag. Trim the end with a piece of paper tape. Add a single sticker. Thread the ribbon through the hole and attach to the top of the box.

Biscotti Wrap
shown on page 68

- purchased food-quality cellophane bag
- rubber band
- one teal and one silver jingle bell
- $3\frac{1}{4}$" x $2\frac{1}{4}$" piece of teal polka dot scrapbook paper
- 6" x 4" piece of 2-sided printed scrapbook paper
- purchased large decorative brad
- glue stick
- adhesive foam dots
- 14" strip of $\frac{1}{4}$" w teal ribbon

1. Place biscotti in cellophane bag and secure with rubber band.
2. For the tag, copy the printed tag (page 150) onto white paper and cut

out. Adhere to the polka dot piece of scrapbook paper. Add the large decorative brad at the corner. Fold the larger piece of scrapbook paper in half. Adhere the message tag to the front using adhesive foam dots.
3. Punch a hole in the corner of the folded tag. Thread the jingle bells onto the ribbon. Thread the ribbon through the hole and tie to the top of the bag.

Berry Scone Mix Jar and Tag
shown on page 69

- quart jar with lid
- 4" x 4" piece of patterned cardstock
- white paper and computer/printer
- scraps of rickrack in desired color
- pinking shears
- crafts glue
- double-stick tape
- 10" piece of baker's twine
- instructions for making the scones printed on a 3"x3" piece of paper (See page 69 for recipe instructions.)

1. Trim the edges of the printed cardstock with pinking shears to make a $3\frac{1}{2}$" x $3\frac{1}{2}$" square. Print "Berry Scone Mix" in desired font to fit a 3"x 3" square. Cut out and adhere to front of patterned cardstock using a glue stick.
2. Adhere scraps of rickrack around the white paper using crafts glue. Tape the ends of the baker's twine to the back of the tag. Adhere the instructions for making the scones on the back over the taped twine using crafts glue. Let dry. Slide the tag over the jar neck.

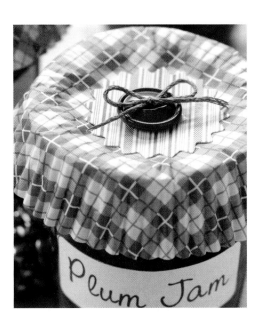

Festive Jam Jar
shown on page 70

- cupcake liner in desired pattern
- scrap of scrapbook paper
- decorative scissors (optional)
- 2-hole button
- 10" piece of embroidery floss in desired color
- scissors
- double-stick tape
- crafts glue
- computer and paper

(continued on page 140)

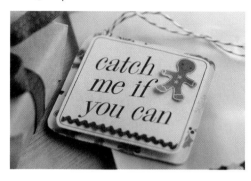

(continued from page 139)

1. Flatten cupcake liner and reposition over the top of the finished jar of jam, centering the liner. Adhere in place with double stick tape. Thread the embroidery floss through the holes in the button and tie a knot and bow. Set aside. Cut a small circle from the scrapbook paper and adhere to the center of the cupcake liner. Adhere the button on top of the paper.

2. Create a label using a computer font and cut out. Adhere to the front of the jar.

Candy Box

shown on page 71

- small box with lid
- small-print scrapbook paper
- length of rickrack to fit around top of box
- scrap of contrasting scrapbook paper
- glue stick
- scissors
- 3"x4" piece of cardstock
- scraps of narrow ribbon
- paper punch
- bakers' twine
- cream-color paper
- computer/printer
- small cupcake liners

1. Cover the box using the printed scrapbook paper, adhering with the glue stick. Adhere the rickrack around the top of the box.

2. To make the tag, adhere scrapbook papers to the tag as desired. Add pieces of narrow ribbon where the papers meet. Print message on cream paper and adhere to tag front. Punch a hole at the corner and thread bakers' twine through the hole. Place candies in small cupcake liners and place in box. Close box and add the tag.

Holiday Bread Wrap

shown on page 72

- purchased printed bandanna with cherry pattern
- wood cutting board
- printed napkin with cherry design
- crafts glue
- white paper
- 2" x 3" scrap of polka dot scrapbook paper
- adhesive foam dots
- transparent tape

1. Place the bread into a cellophane bag and onto the cutting board. Wrap the bandanna around the bread.

2. For tag, copy the printed tag (page 150) onto white paper and cut out. Adhere to the polka dot paper and trim around to make curved corners. Set aside. Glue the layers of the napkin together. Let dry. Cut a

$3^1/2$" x $2^3/4$" piece from the napkin and curve the edges. Adhere the tag to the napkin using adhesive foam dots. Punch hole at one edge of napkin and thread bakers' twine through the hole. Attach the tag to the underside of the cutting board using tape.

Gingerbread Man Envelope and Tag

shown on page 73

For envelope:
- 11" x 7" piece of vellum paper
- decorative scissors
- red paper tape such as Washi tape
- 12" length of red mini rickrack
- 12" length of green checked ribbon
- 3"x3" piece of scrapbook paper
- crafts glue

For tag:
- 3"x3" piece of printed cardstock
- cream-color paper
- adhesive foam dots
- 3" piece of mini rickrack
- paper punch
- scissors
- 12" piece of red/white bakers' twine
- purchased gingerbread man sticker

1. For envelope, fold the paper in half to make a $5^1/2$" x 7" rectangle. On the long sides, fold back each edge $1/2$" and secure with glue. Trim the top of the envelope with decorative scissors. Run a line of glue on the open bottom of the papers and secure with glue. Decorate with paper tape. Adhere the rickrack between the paper tape strips.

2. For tag, copy the printed tag (page 151) onto cream-color paper and cut out. Set aside. Punch a hole at one edge of the cardstock. Fold the bakers' twine in half and thread twine through the hole. Adhere the printed tag to the front of the cardstock using adhesive foam dots. Adhere the tag to the envelope and slide the cookie or cookies into the envelope.

Candy Cane Box and Tag
shown on page 75

- small bakery box with cellophane top
- parchment paper
- printed scrapbook paper in desired print to cover box
- glue stick
- red decorative paper tape such as Washi tape
- purchased circle greeting tag
- decorative brad
- pinking shears
- scrap of red narrow ribbon
- scissors

1. Cut the printed paper to fit the outside of the box. Adhere to the box with glue stick. Embellish the box using decorative paper tape as desired.
2. Cut a 3"x3" piece of patterned paper using pinking shears. Attach the greeting tag to the paper using a decorative brad. Set aside.
3. Line the bakery box with parchment paper. Arrange the candy canes in the box. Close the lid and secure with decorative paper tape. Tape the ribbon to the back of the tag and lay across the top of the box, securing in place with tape.

Croissant Basket and Tag
shown on page 76

- woven basket large enough to hold croissants
- Christmas-print fabric to fit basket
- pinking shears
- 3 $\frac{1}{2}$" x 5" piece of green cardstock
- paper sticker to fit tag
- paper punch
- 8" length of bakers' twine

1. For the basket liner, wash and dry fabric. Iron if necessary. Pink edges of the fabric and tuck into basket.
2. Fold cardstock in half. Adhere sticker to the front of the card. Punch a hole in the corner and thread the twine through the hole. Tie onto basket.

Candy Tag
shown on page 74

- small jar with hinged lid or pint canning jar
- white paper
- 3"x3" piece of red cardstock
- adhesive foam dots
- paper punch
- scissors
- 12" piece of $\frac{1}{4}$" w satin ribbon

1. Arrange the candy pieces in the jar and close the jar.
2. Copy the printed tag (page 151) on white paper and cut out. Set aside. Punch 2 holes at the top of the red cardstock. Thread the satin ribbon through the holes from the back side, knotting the ribbon in the back. Adhere the printed tag to the front of the red cardstock using adhesive foam dots. Slide the tag over the top of the jar.

Vinegar Bottle and Tag
shown on page 77

- glass bottles with hinged lids or corks
- cream-color paper

(continued on page 142)

(continued from page 141)

- scraps of printed scrapbook paper
- scissors
- glue stick
- red and green variegated embroidery floss
- crafts glue

1. Copy the printed tags (page 151) on cream-color paper and cut out. Cut a piece of printed scrapbook paper slightly larger than the printed tags. Cut out. Adhere the tag to the front of the scrapbook paper using a glue stick. Poke a small hole at each corner of the tag. Cut a 9" piece of embroidery floss. Using all 6 strands, thread through the holes for hanging. Set aside.
2. Wrap the necks of the bottles with embroidery floss using all 6 strands while wrapping. Secure the ends with crafts glue. Hang a tag over the neck of each bottle.

Reindeer Food Mix Wrap and Tag
shown on page 78

- purchased Santa hat
- cellophane treat bag
- white paper
- adhesive foam dots

- 2¹/₂" x 3¹/₂" piece of red cardstock
- 1¹/₂" x 3" piece of patterned cardstock
- glue stick
- red embroidery floss
- paper punch

1. To make tag, copy the printed oval (page 151) on white paper and cut out. Set aside.
2. Punch 2 holes at the top of the red cardstock. Adhere the patterned cardstock to the top front of the red cardstock. Adhere the oval tag near the bottom of the red cardstock using an adhesive foam dot.
3. Thread the embroidery floss through the holes from the back side knotting the floss in the back. Place the treat mix in the cellophane and secure with a small piece of ribbon. Tuck the bag into the Santa hat. Place tag on hat.

Cake Mix Jar and Tag
shown on page 79

- quart jar with lid
- glue and water mixture (1 T. white tacky glue and 1 T. water)
- paintbrush

- 3" x 6" piece of patterned cardstock
- scrap of red cardstock
- decorative brad
- white paper
- computer printer
- crafts glue
- pinking shears
- 12" piece of bakers' twine
- instructions for making the cake printed on a 2³/₄" x 2³/₄" piece of paper (See page 79 for recipe instructions.)
- 12" piece of ¹/₂" w brown-and-white ribbon

1. Be sure the jar is clean and dry. For jar label, copy the art (page 151) onto white paper and cut out carefully. Use the paintbrush to paint the glue and water mixture on the back of the label. Carefully position it on the jar and rub with your finger. Add another coat of the glue and water mixture on top of the label painting the mixture just past the edges of the paper. Let dry.
2. For the tag, fold the printed scrapbook paper in half. Trim the edge with pinking shears. Print out the message in desired font, cut out and adhere to scrap of red paper. Curve the edges. Use a decorative brad to attach to the front of the tag. Punch a hole in the tag and thread the bakers' twine through the hole. Glue the instructions for making the cake inside the tag. Place mix in the jar, and put lid on top. Tie the checked ribbon and tag around the jar.

General Instructions

Making Patterns

When the entire pattern is shown, place tracing or tissue paper over the pattern and draw over the lines. For a more durable pattern, use a permanent marker to draw over the pattern on stencil plastic—this is sometimes also called a template.

When only half of the pattern is shown (indicated by a dotted line on the pattern), fold the tracing paper in half. Place the fold along the dotted line and trace the pattern half. Turn the folded paper over and draw over the traced lines on the remaining side. Unfold the pattern and cut it out.

Sizing Patterns

To change the size of the pattern, divide the desired height or width of the pattern (whichever is greater) by the actual height or width of the pattern. Multiply the result by 100 and photocopy the pattern at this percentage.

For example: You want your pattern to be 8"h, but the pattern on the page is 6" h. So 8:6=1.33x100=133%. Copy the pattern at 133%.

If your copier doesn't enlarge to the size you need, enlarge the pattern to the maximum percentage on the copier. Then repeat step 1, dividing the desired size by the size of the enlarged pattern. Multiply this result by 100 and photocopy the enlarged pattern at the new percentage.

For very large projects, you'll need to enlarge the design in sections onto separate sheets of paper. Repeat as needed to reach the desired size and tape the pattern pieces together.

Transferring Patterns to Fabrics

Enlarge the pattern if necessary. Trace the pattern onto tissue paper. Pin the tissue paper to the fabric and stitch through the paper along the pattern lines. Carefully tear the tissue paper away. Or, pin the pattern to the fabric and cut around the pattern pieces.

TRANSFERRING PATTERNS TO CARDSTOCK OR OTHER MATERIALS

Trace the pattern onto tracing paper. Place the pattern on the cardstock (or whatever material you are transferring to) and use a pencil to lightly draw around the pattern. For pattern details, slip transfer paper between the pattern and the cardstock and draw over the detail lines.

Cutting a Stencil

Enlarge the pattern if necessary. Using a fine-point permanent marker, trace the pattern onto stencil plastic or mylar. Carefully cut the plastic with scissors or a crafts knife, making sure all edges are smooth.

To paint with a stencil, use only a little paint on the stencil brush. Then use an up-and-down motion when painting. Remove the stencil immediately after painting.

Making a Fabric Circle

Matching right sides, fold the fabric square in half from top to bottom and again from left to right. Tie one end of a length of string to a water-soluble marking pen; insert a thumbtack through the string at the length indicated in the project instructions. Insert the thumbtack through the folded corner of the fabric. Holding the tack in place and keeping the string taut, mark the cutting line (Fig. 1).

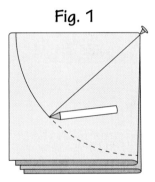

Fig. 1

Embroidery Stitches

Always come up at 1 and all odd numbers and go down at 2 and all even numbers unless otherwise indicated.

BACKSTITCH

Bring the needle up at 1, go down at 2, come up at 3 and go down at 4 (Fig. 2).

Fig. 2

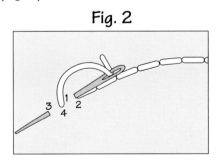

BLANKET STITCH

Referring to Fig. 3, bring the needle up at 1. Keeping the thread below the point of the needle, go down at 2 and come up at 3. Continue working as shown in Fig. 4.

Fig. 3

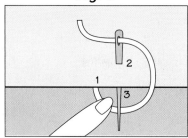

Fig. 4

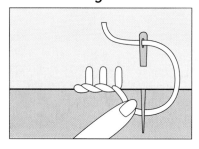

BULLION KNOT

Referring to Fig. 5, bring the needle up at 1 and take the needle down at 2 (this is the distance the knot will cover); come up at 1 again and wrap the yarn around the needle as many times as necessary to cover the distance between 1 and 2. Pull needle through wraps and adjust on the 1-2 loop (Figs. 6-7).

Fig. 5

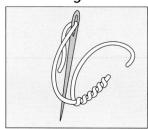

Fig. 6

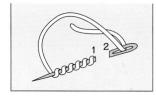

Fig. 7

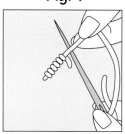

Anchor the knot with a small straight stitch at 2 (Fig. 8).

Fig. 8

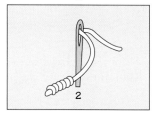

CHAIN STITCH

Referring to Fig. 9, bring the needle up at 1; take the needle down again at 1 to form a loop. Bring the needle up at 2; take the needle down again at 2 to form a second loop (Fig. 10). Continue making loops. Anchor the last chain with a small straight stitch (Fig. 11).

Fig. 9

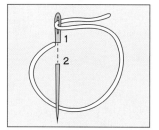

Fig. 10

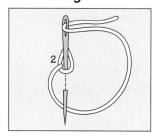

Fig. 11

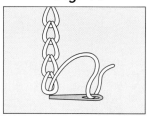

COUCHING STITCH

Referring to Fig. 12, lay the thread to be couched on the fabric; bring the needle up at 1 and go down at 2. Continue until entire thread length is couched.

Fig. 12

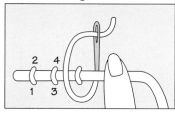

CROSS STITCH

Bring the needle up at 1 and go down at 2. Come up at 3 and go down at 4 (Fig. 13).

Fig. 13

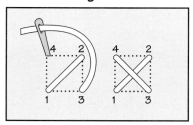

For the horizontal rows, work the stitches in 2 journeys (Fig. 14).

Fig. 14

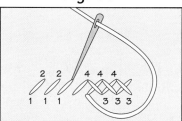

FERN STITCH

Referring to Fig. 15, work the central spine first then stitch a straight stitch either side of that spine. Bring needle up at 1, down at 2, up at 3, down at 4 and up at 5.

Fig. 15

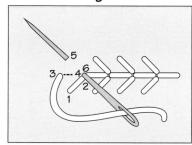

Fly Stitch

Refer to Fig. 16. Fly Stitch is also known as "Y" Stitch. It is worked making a V-shaped loop which is then tied down by a vertical Straight Stitch. Bring needle through the fabric out at the top and to the left of the line that is to be worked.

Fig. 16

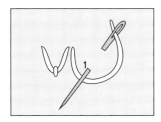

French Knot

Referring to Fig. 17, bring the needle up at 1. Wrap the floss once around the needle and insert the needle at 2, holding the floss end with non-stitching fingers. Tighten the knot; then, pull the needle through the fabric, holding the floss until it must be released. For larger knot, use more strands; wrap only once.

Fig. 17

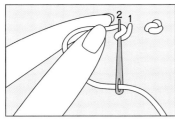

Lazy Daisy

Bring the needle up at 1; take the needle back down at 1 to form a loop and bring the needle up at 2. Keeping the loop below the point of the needle (Fig. 18), take the needle down at 3 to anchor the loop.

Fig. 18

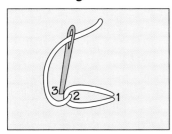

Running Stitch

Referring to Fig. 19, make a series of straight stitches with the stitch length equal to the space between stitches.

Fig. 19

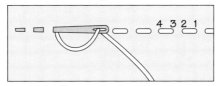

Stem Stitch

Referring to Fig. 20, come up at 1. Keeping the thread below the stitching line, go down at 2 and come up at 3. Go down at 4 and come up at 5.

Fig. 20

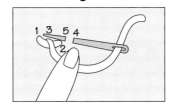

Straight Stitch

Referring to Fig. 21, come up at 1 and go down at 2.

Fig. 21

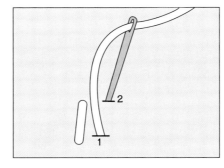

Pom-poms

For a 2" diameter pom-pom, place an 8" piece of yarn along one long edge of a 1"x3" cardboard strip. Wrap yarn around and around the strip and yarn piece (Fig. 22). (The more you wrap, the fluffier the pom-pom.) Tie the wound yarn together tightly with the 8" piece. Leaving the tie ends long to attach the pom-pom, cut the loops opposite the tie; then, fluff and trim the pom-pom into a smooth ball.

Fig. 22

Crochet Abbreviations

Abbreviations

ch(s)	chain(s)
cm	centimeters
dc	double crochet
hdc	half double crochet
lp(s)	loop(s)
mm	millimeters
sl st	slip stitch
sc(s)	single crochet(s)
st(s)	stitch(es)
tr	treble crochet

*—work instructions following * as many **more** times as indicated in addition to the first time. *

( ) or [ ] — contains explanatory remarks

colon (:) — the number given after a colon at the end of a row denotes the number of stitches you should have on that row.

Gauge

Exact gauge is essential for proper fit. Before beginning your project, make a sample swatch in the yarn and hook specified. After completing the swatch, measure it, counting your stitches and rows or rounds carefully. If your swatch is larger or smaller than specified, make another, changing hook size to get the correct gauge. Keep trying until you find the size hook that will give you the specified gauge.

Patterns

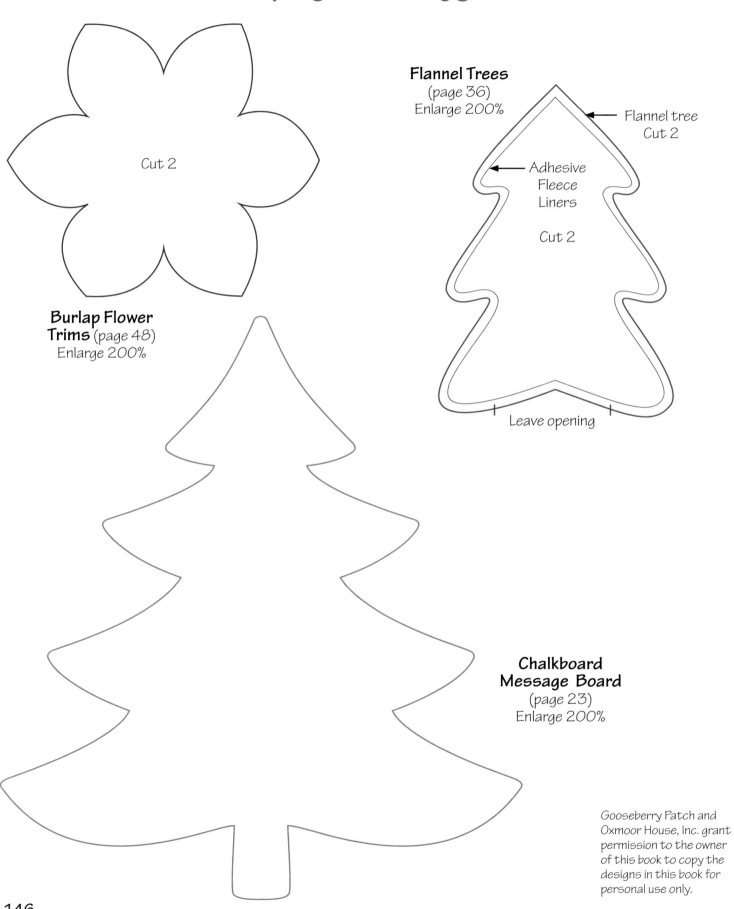

Flannel Trees
(page 36)
Enlarge 200%

Flannel tree
Cut 2

Adhesive
Fleece
Liners

Cut 2

Leave opening

Cut 2

**Burlap Flower
Trims** (page 48)
Enlarge 200%

**Chalkboard
Message Board**
(page 23)
Enlarge 200%

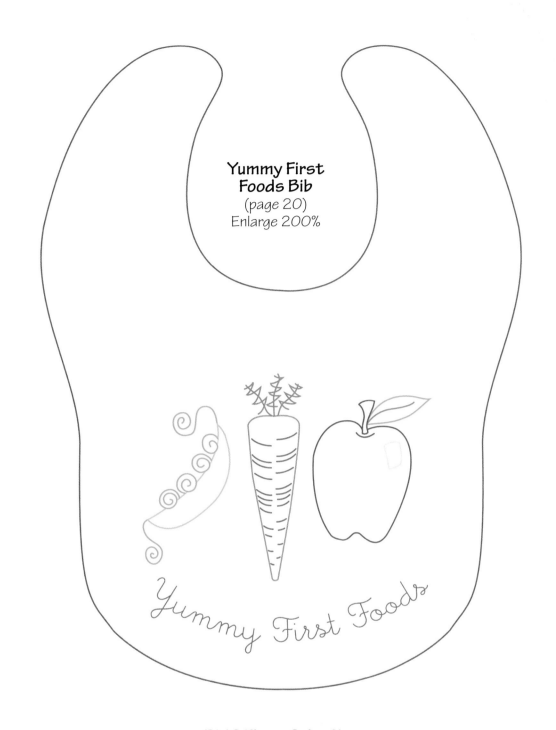

**Yummy First
Foods Bib**
(page 20)
Enlarge 200%

DMC Floss Color Key

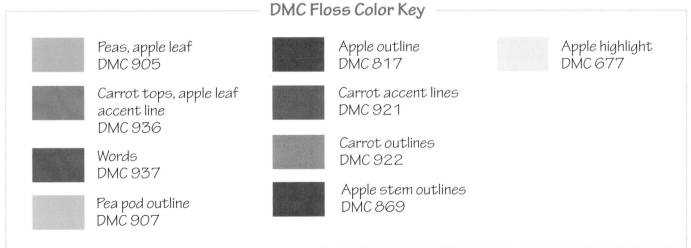

Peas, apple leaf
DMC 905

Carrot tops, apple leaf
accent line
DMC 936

Words
DMC 937

Pea pod outline
DMC 907

Apple outline
DMC 817

Carrot accent lines
DMC 921

Carrot outlines
DMC 922

Apple stem outlines
DMC 869

Apple highlight
DMC 677

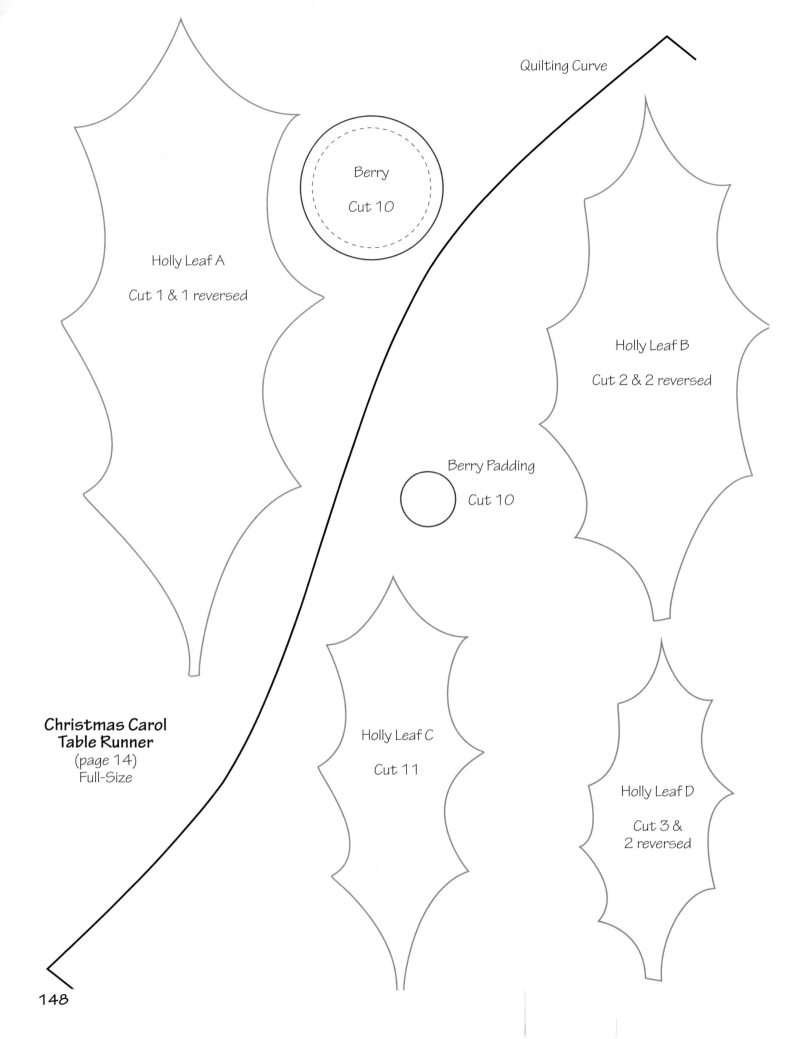

Quilting Curve

Berry

Cut 10

Holly Leaf A

Cut 1 & 1 reversed

Holly Leaf B

Cut 2 & 2 reversed

Berry Padding

Cut 10

**Christmas Carol
Table Runner**
(page 14)
Full-Size

Holly Leaf C

Cut 11

Holly Leaf D

Cut 3 &
2 reversed

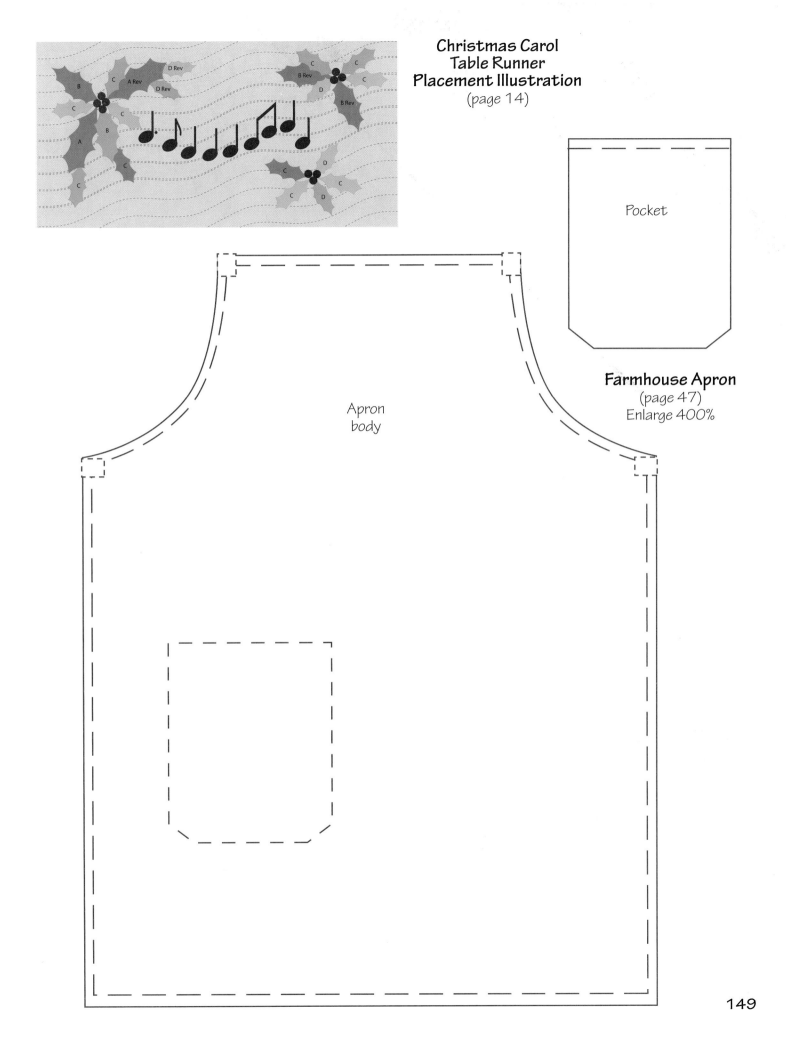

Christmas Carol
Table Runner
Placement Illustration
(page 14)

Pocket

Apron
body

Farmhouse Apron
(page 47)
Enlarge 400%

149

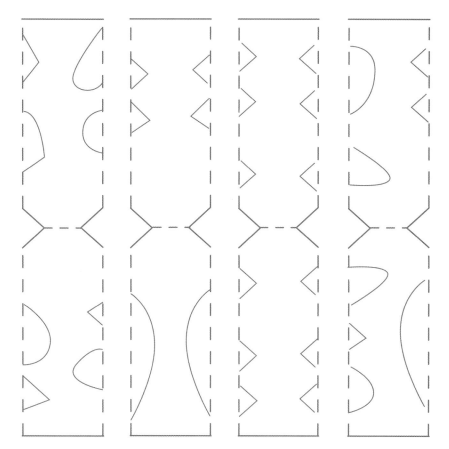

Lacy Snowflakes
(page 12)
Full-Size

Happy
Holidays

Merry
Christmas

**Merry
Christmas**

**Goodies from
the Kitchen Tags**
(pages 65–79)
Full-Size

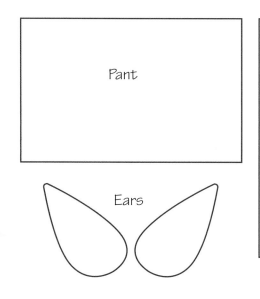

Pant

Ears

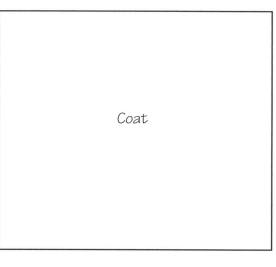

Coat

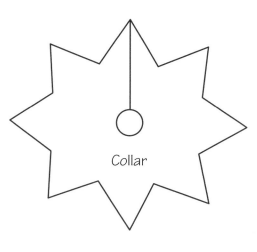

Collar

**Happy Clothespin
Elves** (page 61)
Full-Size

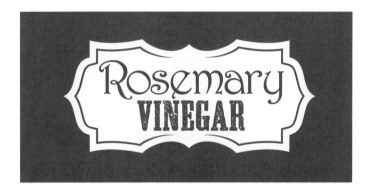

Goodies from the Kitchen Tags
(pages 65–79)
Full-Size

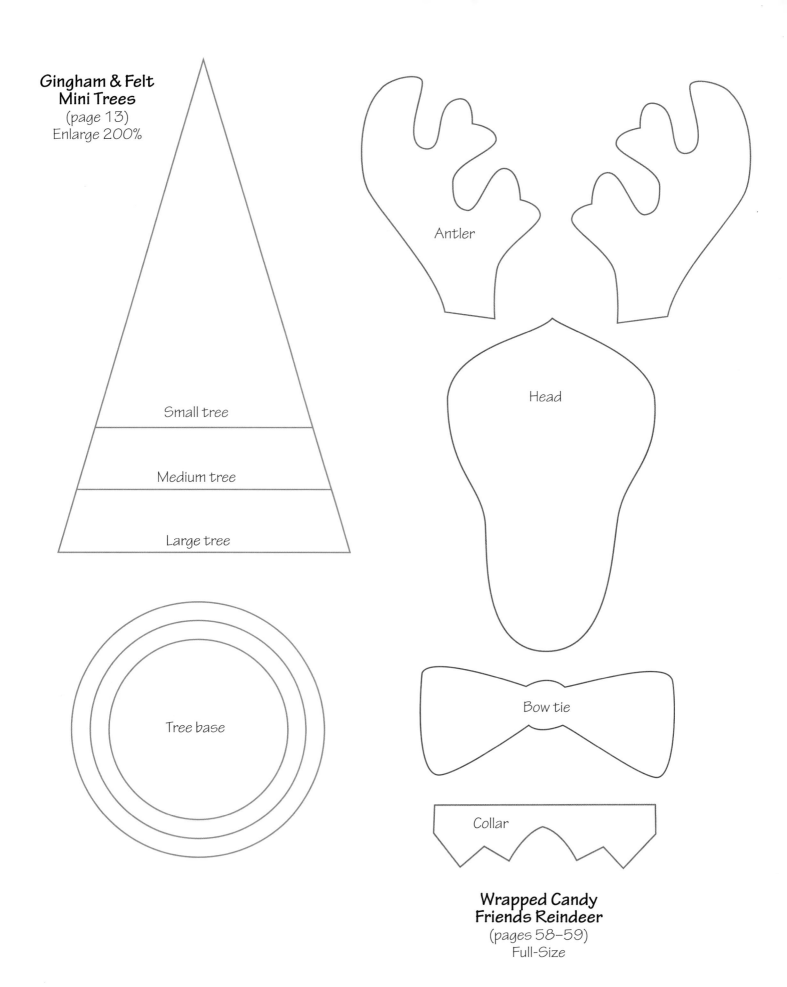

Gingham & Felt Mini Trees
(page 13)
Enlarge 200%

Small tree

Medium tree

Large tree

Tree base

Antler

Head

Bow tie

Collar

Wrapped Candy Friends Reindeer
(pages 58–59)
Full-Size

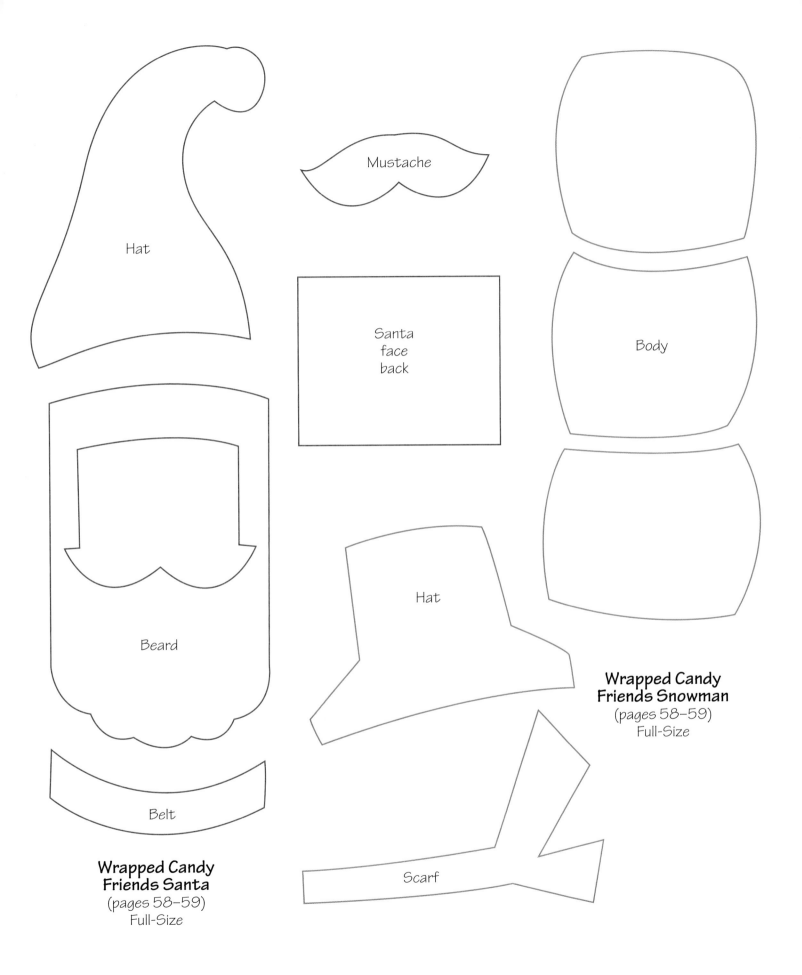

Mustache

Hat

Santa
face
back

Body

Beard

Hat

Belt

Wrapped Candy
Friends Snowman
(pages 58–59)
Full-Size

Scarf

**Wrapped Candy
Friends Santa**
(pages 58–59)
Full-Size

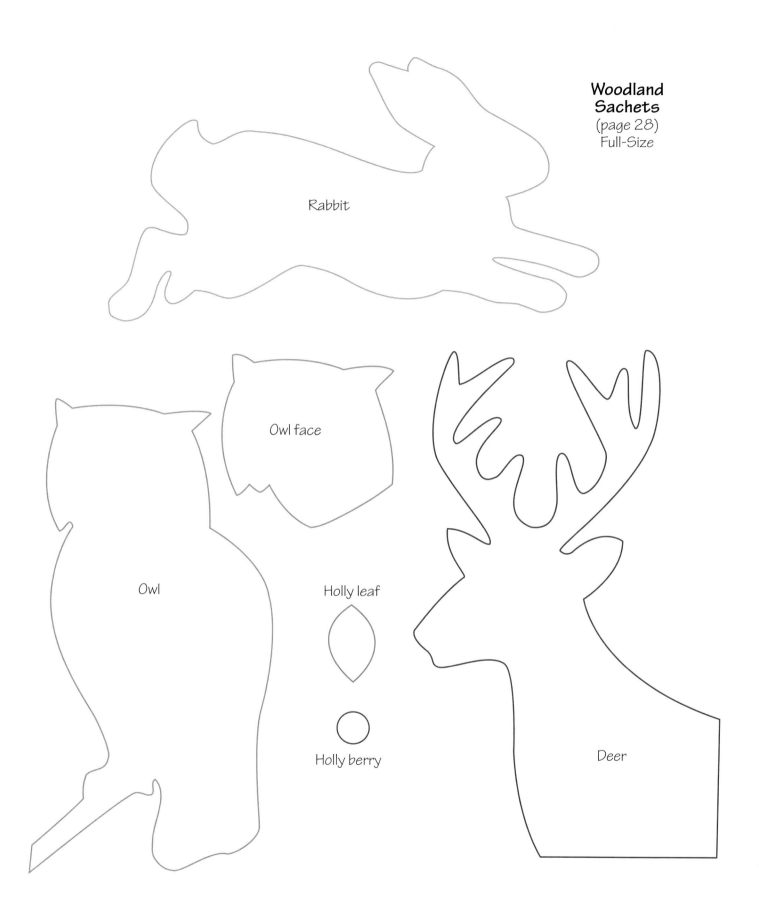

Rabbit

Owl face

Owl

Holly leaf

Holly berry

Deer

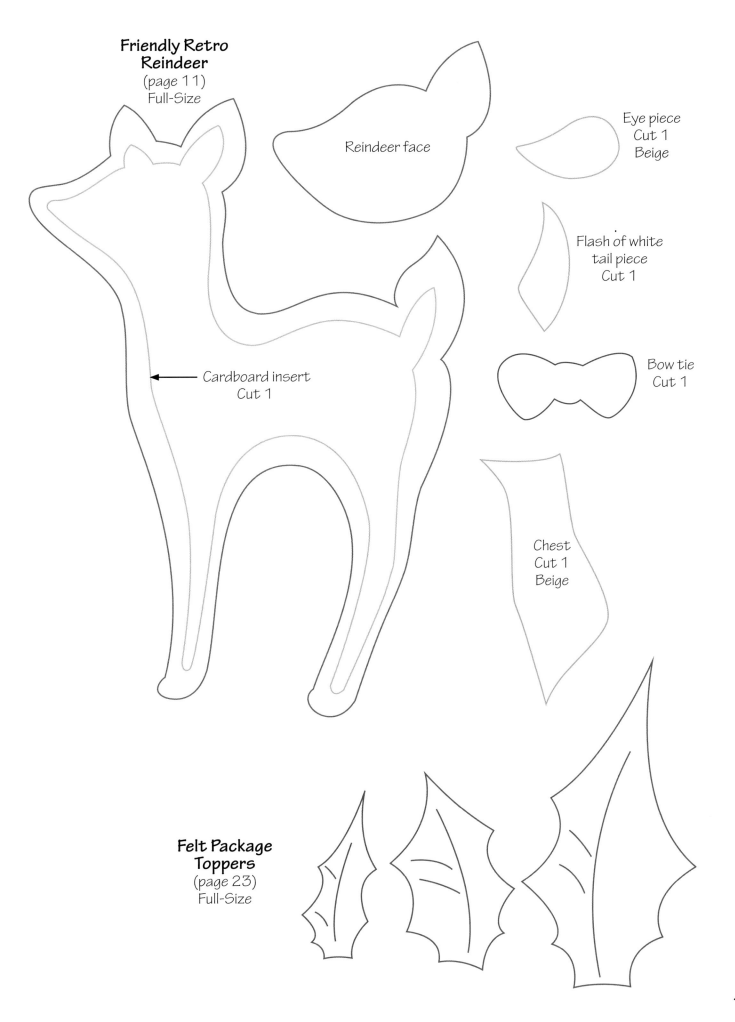

Friendly Retro Reindeer
(page 11)
Full-Size

Reindeer face

Eye piece
Cut 1
Beige

Flash of white
tail piece
Cut 1

Cardboard insert
Cut 1

Bow tie
Cut 1

Chest
Cut 1
Beige

Felt Package Toppers
(page 23)
Full-Size

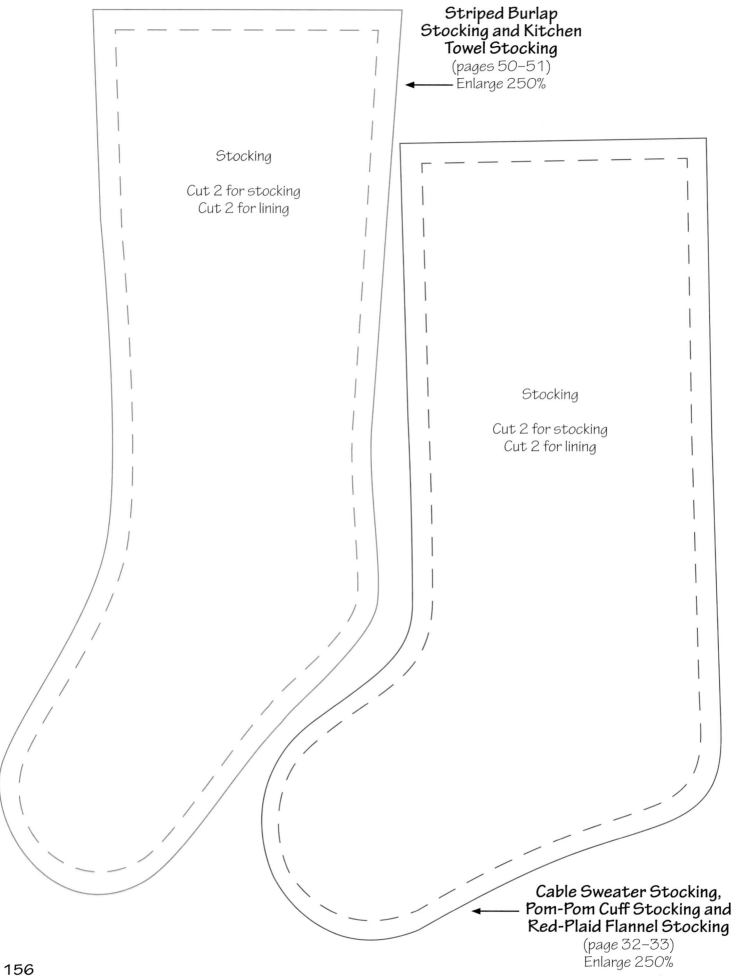

**Striped Burlap
Stocking and Kitchen
Towel Stocking**
(pages 50–51)
Enlarge 250%

Stocking

Cut 2 for stocking
Cut 2 for lining

Stocking

Cut 2 for stocking
Cut 2 for lining

**Cable Sweater Stocking,
Pom-Pom Cuff Stocking and
Red-Plaid Flannel Stocking**
(page 32–33)
Enlarge 250%

**12 Days of Christmas
Kitchen Towel Set**
(pages 54–55)
Enlarge 150%

DMC Floss Color Key

DMC 986	DMC 321	DMC 3822
DMC 989	DMC 420	DMC 518

Project Index

Clothing & Accessories
Cheery Cherry Tote Bag, 19
Farmhouse Apron, 47
Foxy Baby Hat, 21
Grandmother's Beaded Bracelet, 22
Yummy First Foods Bib, 20

Food Gift Packaging
Berry Scone Mix Jar and Tag, 69
Biscotti Wrap, 68
Cake Jar and Tag, 79
Candy Box, 71
Candy Cane Box and Tag, 75
Candy Tag, 74
Croissant Basket and Tag, 76
Festive Jam Jar, 70
Gingerbread Man Envelope and Tag, 73
Holiday Bread Wrap, 72
Mix Wrap and Tag, 78
Pretty Cookie Bar Box, 67
Swirl Cookie Pop Bag, 65
Vinegar Bottle and Tags, 77

Gift Tags, Cards & Wraps
Buttons & Bows Wraps, 22
Color-Etched Greeting Cards, 62
Easy Sticker Cards, 40
Evergreen Print Greeting Cards, 29
Felt Package Toppers, 23

Gifts
Chalkboard Message Board, 23
Cheery Cherry Tote Bag, 19
Fingerprint Tree Hot Pad, 63
Foxy Baby Hat, 21

Handprint Hot Pads, 63
Heart Handprint Hot Pad, 63
Lacy Handprint Hot Pad, 63
Yummy First Foods Bib, 20

Home Décor & Accessories
12 Days of Christmas Kitchen Towels, 54-55
Argyle Sweater Pillow, 34
Bracelet Candle Centerpiece, 41
Buche De Noel, 27
Burlap & Berry Wreath, 45
Canning Jar Candles, 53
Carved Evergreen Candles, 17
Christmas Carol Table Runner, 14
Christmas Lights Candle, 43
Christmas Package Bookends, 42
Clever Candle Surrounds, 43
Country Welcome Pillow, 49
Evergreen Welcome, 15
Fluffy Flannel Wreath, 33
Fun Cupcake Liner Wreath, 57
Gingham & Felt Mini Trees, 13
Lyrical Pillows, 40
Oil Cloth Table Topper, 46
Painted Plaid Vase, 37
Rickrack Place Mat, 16
Sweet Music Napkin Ring, 17
Vintage Button Candle, 43
Woven Denim Place Mat, 52

Kid Stuff
Candy Wrapped Friends, 58
Candy Wrapped Reindeer, 59
Candy Wrapped Santa, 59

Candy Wrapped Snowman, 58
Color-Etched Greeting Cards, 62
Fingerprint Tree Hot Pad, 63
Fun Cupcake Liner Wreath, 57
Handprint Hot Pads, 63
Happy Clothespin Elves, 61
Heart Handprint Hot Pad, 63
Lacy Handprint Hot Pad, 63
Little Drummer Boy Drums, 60

Outdoor Inspired Décor
Buche De Noel, 27
Evergreen Print Greeting Cards, 29
Icy Wreaths, 26
Message Rocks, 29
Sticks & Stones Swag, 26
Woodland Sachets, 28

Tree Trimmings & Stockings
Burlap Flower Trims, 48
Cable Sweater Stocking, 32
Flannel Tree Trio, 36
Friendly Retro Reindeer, 11
Kitchen Towel Stocking, 51
Lacy Snowflakes, 12
Little Drummer Boy Drums, 60
Music-Inspired Paper Chain, 12
Pom-Pom Cuff Stocking, 32
Pom-pom Garland, 10
Pom-pom Package Trim, 10
Popcorn Candles, 43
Pretty Plaid Boxes, 35
Red-Plaid Flannel Stocking, 31
Striped Burlap Stocking, 50
Sweet Candy Garland, 61

Credits

We want to extend a warm "thank you!" to so many people who helped to create this book:

We want to thank Jay Wilde at The Wilde Project and Dean Tanner at Primary Image for sharing their excellent photographic skills with us. We also want to thank Jennifer Peterson for sharing her beautiful food art talents with us!

It takes quality supplies to make beautiful projects. These are some of the companies that we used to make the crafts and decorating projects in the book: DMC Corporation for embroidery floss, Bazzill Basics for many of the paper crafts, National Nonwovens for superior felt supplies, Bobs Candies for candy sticks and canes and Red Heart yarn for yarns.

Thank you to Jack Miller Tree Farm and Goode Greenhouse in Des Moines, Iowa, for the beautiful Christmas trees, fresh greenery and wreaths we used in the photos.

Recipe Index

Appetizers, Beverages & Snacks
Christmas Eggnog, 124
Christmas Eve Wassail, 87
Figgy Tapenade, 124
Mississippi Fun Dip, 125
Pepper Corn Cups, 122
Pine Cone Cheese Ball, 121
Shrimp Puffs, 127
Spicy Party Chicken Wings, 123
Spinach-Parmesan Balls, 125
Stuffed Mushrooms, 122

Bread & Rolls
Abigail's Crusty White Bread, 108
Belle's Yeast Rolls, 99
Berry Scone Mix, 69
Best-Ever Italian Bread, 81
Buttermilk Cinnamon Rolls, 110
Cherry & Apple Bread, 72
Chicky Popovers, 127
Christmas Croissants, 76
Cranberry Upside-Down Muffins, 111
Easy Oatmeal Rolls, 107
Party Bubble Bread, 110
Southern Hushpuppies, 109

Cakes & Desserts
Bow-Toped Chocolate Red Wine
   Cupcakes, 94
Buttermilk Pear Cobbler, 115
Cherries Jubilee Crisp, 114
Chocolate-Peanut Butter Marble
   Cupcakes, 93
Golden Cupcakes with Frosted Tree
   Tops, 90
Holiday Cranberry Trifle, 113

Holly-Topped White Cupcakes, 95
Lemon Upside-Down Cake, 105
Peppermint 7-Layer Cake, 118
Pretty Pastel Oatmeal Cupcakes, 92
Upside-Down Apple-Pecan Pie, 117
Yummy Chocolate Cake Mix, 79

Candies & Confections
Best-Ever Bakery Frosting, 90
Cream Cheese Frosting, 119
Bitter Chocolate Frosting, 95
Cool & Creamy Peppermint Fudge, 71
Merry Mocha Frosting, 91
Orange Swirl Fudge, 71
Peanut Butter Frosting, 93
Peppermint Candy Canes, 75
Powdered Sugar Frosting, 73
Reindeer Food, 78
Stained Glass Candy, 74
White Chocolate Buttercream
   Frosting, 93

Condiments, Mixes & Sauces
Fruity Raspberry Vinegar, 77
Plum Jam, 70
Rosemary Vinegar, 77
Vinaigrette Dressing, 102

Cookies & Bars
Christmas Cookie Pops, 65
Christmas Fruit Bars, 66
Holiday Jam Cookies, 87
Holly Cookies, 86
Minty Cheesecake Bars, 67
Old-Fashioned Sugar Cookies, 116
Orange Gingerbread Cut-Outs, 73
Orangy-Ginger Biscotti, 68
Pistachio Wreath Cookies, 114
Quick & Easy Lemon Bars, 66

Entrées
Festive Fireside Meatballs, 126
Herbed Roast Turkey Breast, 97
Honeyed Raspberry Pork Chops, 103
Seafood Lovers' Lasagna, 85

Salads & Soups
Black Cherry Cranberry Salad, 83
Cheesy Chicken Chowder, 83
Chili with Corn Dumplings, 82
Chopped Tomato Salad, 102
Curried Pumpkin Bisque, 81
Honeyed Mango Salad, 104
Irene's Layered Salad, 84
Winter Fruit Salad, 101

Side Dishes & Casseroles
Cheesy Scalloped Potatoes, 100
Creamy Broccoli Casserole, 101
Crunchy Hasselback Potatoes, 100
Easy Baked Corn, 101
Grandma's Holiday Stuffing, 98
Italian Zucchini Bake, 103
Sunshine Carrots, 99

TICKle YOUR MIND. - LINDSEY COLLIER -

Book 16

Content and Artwork by
Gooseberry Patch Company

BRAVE INK PRESS

EDITORIAL STAFF
President and Editorial Director:
Carol Field Dahlstrom
Art Director:
Lyne Neymeyer
Photo Stylists: Carol Dahlstrom, Jennifer Peterson,
Jan Temeyer
Craft Designers: Judy Bailey, Heidi Boyd,
Sonja Carmon, Pam Koelling, Katie LaPorte,
Janet Pittman, Jan Temeyer
Director, Test Kitchens: Jennifer Peterson
Test Kitchens Professionals: Holly Wiederin,
Barbara Hoover
Copy Editor: Elizabeth Burnley
Photography: The Wilde Project, Jay Wilde;
Primary Image, Dean Tanner
Video/Communications: Dr. Michael Dahlstrom

BUSINESS STAFF
Business Manager: Judy Bailey
Webmaster: Leigha Bitz
Production Manager: Dave Hollingsworth
Props/Studio Manager: Roger H. Dahlstrom
Locations: Sharon and Craig Northhouse,
Jan Temeyer
Marketing/Social Media Manager:
Marcia Schultz Dahlstrom

OXMOOR HOUSE
Vice President, Brand Publishing: Laura Sappington
Editorial Director: Leah McLaughlin
Creative Director: Felicity Keane
Brand Manager: Vanessa Tiongson
Senior Editor: Rebecca Brennan
Managing Editor: Elizabeth Austin
Assistant Managing Editor: Jeanne de Lathouder

Gooseberry Patch Christmas Book 16
Editor: Susan Ray
Art Director: Christopher Rhoads
Executive Food Director: Grace Parisi

CONTRIBUTOR
Project Editor: Laura Medlin

TIME HOME ENTERTAINMENT INC.
President and Publisher: Jim Childs
Vice President, Brand & Digital Strategy:
Steven Sandonato
Vice President, Finance: Vandana Patel
Executive Director, Marketing Services: Carol Pittard
Executive Director, Retail & Special Sales: Tom Mifsud
Executive Publishing Director: Joy Butts
Publishing Director: Megan Pearlman
Director, Bookazine Development & Marketing:
Laura Adam
Associate General Counsel: Helen Wan

©2014 by Gooseberry Patch, 2545 Farmers Dr., Ste. 380, Columbus,
OH 43235 1-800-854-6673, gooseberrypatch.com ©2014 by Time
Home Entertainment Inc., 135 West 50th Street, New York, New York
10020.

Hardcover ISSN: 2154-4263
Softcover ISSN: 2154-4263
Hardcover ISBN: 10: 0-8487-0441-X and 0-8487-0438-X
Hardcover ISBN: 13: 978-0-8487-0441-4 and 978-0-8487-0438-4
Softcover ISBN: 10: 0-8487-0439-8
Softcover ISBN: 13: 978-0-8487-0439-1

Printed in the United States of America
First printing 2014